Praise for Ron Pevny's

CONSCIOUS LIVING
CONSCIOUS AGING

"For those entering the second half of life, aging can be the great unknown. Ron Pevny's book is a much-needed map of the territory and an exciting picture of what conscious aging can be all about."
—**Harry R. Moody**, retired Vice President, AARP
and author of *The Five Stages of the Soul*

"This powerful book helps both women and men age purposefully. Read this book and you will experience aging in a whole new way."
—**Richard J. Leider**, bestselling author of *The Power of Purpose*, *Repacking Your Bags*, and *Life Reimagined*

"Ron Pevny's spot-on wisdom on the elegance of aging is spiritually relevant and deeply useful. His is an inspiring voice for living in greater mindfulness within each present moment."
—**Michael Bernard Beckwith**, author of *Life Visioning*

CONSCIOUS LIVING

CONSCIOUS AGING

embrace & savor your next chapter

RON PEVNY

ATRIA PAPERBACK
New York London Toronto Sydney New Delhi

BEYOND WORDS
Hillsboro, Oregon

 PAPERBACK
A Division of Simon & Schuster, Inc.
1230 Avenue of the Americas
New York, NY 10020

BEYOND WORDS
20827 N.W. Cornell Road, Suite 500
Hillsboro, Oregon 97124-9808
503-531-8700 / 503-531-8773 fax
www.beyondword.com

Managing editor: Lindsay S. Brown
Editors: Emily Han, Sarah Heilman, Emmalisa Sparrow
Copyeditor: Claire Rudy Foster
Proofreader: Jade Chan
Design: Devon Smith
Composition: William H. Brunson Typography Services

First Atria Paperback/Beyond Words trade paperback edition October 2014

Library of Congress Cataloging-in-Publication Data

Pevny, Ron.
    Conscious living, conscious aging : embrace & savor your next chapter / Ron Pevny.
        pages cm
    Includes bibliographical references.
        1. Retirement.   2. Retirement—Planning.   3. Retirees—Life skills guides.   4. Older people—Conduct of life.   5. Aging—Social aspects.   I. Title.
HQ1062.P485   2014
306.3'8—dc23

                                                                                                2014009041

    ISBN 978-1-58270-438-8
    ISBN 978-1-4767-2963-3 (eBook)

The corporate mission of Beyond Words Publishing, Inc.: *Inspire to Integrity*

CONTENTS

CONTENTS

PREFACE

The greatest danger for most of us is not that our aim is too high
and we miss it, but that it is too low and we reach it.

—MICHELANGELO

What do you aim for as you age? This book is for the millions of baby boomers in or nearing their sixties and older adults for whom this and related questions feel significant. Among these questions are, What does aging mean to me? How do I deal with my fears of aging? How can I find fulfillment and dignity as I age? What is the purpose of my life after retirement? Such questions of meaning and purpose arise in our quiet moments but are seldom addressed in public. Modern culture often only considers the monetary aspect of aging. While acknowledging our need for financial and physical security is certainly important, it is equally important to fulfill the needs of our emotional and spiritual selves—our desire to thrive as well as survive. This book is a resource for addressing these questions as you gain awareness of what is possible for you and learn how you

can live into these potentials. This book is about aging with awareness and intention rather than merely growing old; it's about aging
consciously.

Although my primary life's work has focused on assisting people as they negotiate and grow through life transitions, aging did not
appear on my personal and professional radar until I reached my fifties. At that time, two catalysts, both personally and professionally,
led me onto the path of conscious aging. I began to do video-based
oral history work with my parents and other older relatives and with
seniors in the hospice and reminiscence programs in my community of Durango, Colorado. As I worked, I found myself more and
more intrigued with hearing others' life stories. I imagined what my
life would be like when I reached elderhood. In 2001 two wise elders,
Wes Burwell and Ann Roberts, asked me to help create a program
that would serve as a rite of passage onto the path of conscious aging.
Together we designed the first Choosing Conscious Elderhood retreats.
Wes and Ann served as powerful models for conscious elderhood,
and I contributed my extensive experience in guiding rites of passage.

These catalysts pointed me toward my calling for this stage of
my life. My trajectory solidified a few years later when my life was
shaken to the core as I neared sixty and had my first encounter with
my mortality. I began experiencing the first of many frightening
heart arrhythmias, which were "probably" related to a large tumor
discovered in my right lung. The ten-day wait for my biopsy results
was probably the most powerful growth experience of my life. It was
a time of fear alternating with a trust that seemed to be arising from
somewhere deeper than my chaotic emotional self. I became acutely
aware of unfinished business with others, myself, and my creator.
For the first time I felt strong empathy—grounded in personal experience—for the vulnerability, fear, loss, confusion, and hope that are

part of the aging process for most of us. I found that my greatest fear was not that I would die but that I would die before I fulfilled the calling my life had been preparing me for.

To the surprise of the pulmonary specialists, the tumor was not malignant but a rare benign mass. It still needed immediate, delicate surgical removal. After four days in the hospital, I went home and was greatly distressed; the heart arrhythmias continued, as frequent and frightening as ever. On the third or fourth night, as sleep eluded me due to my strange heart rhythms, I entered a dream or trance state. I felt myself being overtaken and smothered by a dark energy, which was death itself. All I could do was surrender, acknowledging that there was nothing else I could do to be healed and asking the Divine to help me. At that moment, I felt the darkness explode out of me. I awoke knowing that significant healing had occurred. That powerful affirmation marked the end of the heart arrhythmias and the beginning of a new stage in my personal conscious eldering work and my work as a guide for others on this path.

What I learned through that experience plays a key role in what I teach in the retreats and workshops offered by my Center for Conscious Eldering, which I founded in 2010, and what I share with you in this book. This personal journey has taught me that helping people answer the question, "What do you aim for as you age?" enables me to grow, be fulfilled, and serve others in the elder third of my life.

The fire of my passion for this calling has been fueled by the passionate retreat and workshop attendants, most of whom have a sense of urgency to answer those big questions. These people are in their fifties, sixties, seventies, and even eighties. They are facing the challenge of creating an elderhood with meaning, passion, growth, and service. This is daunting because our world offers little that is high and noble after retirement. It tells us that the last two or three decades of our precious lives have no societally valued role or purpose. These participants have deeply inspired me. I have also been greatly blessed to have wise conscious elders in my life who have served as mentors and colleagues. They have taught me much as they courageously followed their call to live with meaning and growth as their goals. I have learned that making the effort to prepare well, in a way that reflects our individual needs and temperaments, is critical to finding the fulfillment that is possible. There is a difference between simply drifting into old age and aging consciously with intention. For those who feel called to conscious elderhood, preparation is necessary—the sooner the better.

This book is written for aging people who have a sense (clear or not) of the possibilities for purpose, growth, and service that lie ahead. For some readers, this sense may be little more than a vague aching or yearning for something *more* than what modern culture currently offers. Others may have a strong sense of calling accompanied by a need for guidance. Either way, it's a journey with few cultural maps and landmarks. I cannot offer a prescription that guarantees your full potential for joy as you age. I cannot tell you how to allow the elder energy seeking expression through you to best shine forth. What I can do is offer perspectives, strategies, practices, rituals, and stories to help you do the inner work. This book will help you prepare to shine your elder light as brightly as possible during the life chapters that lie ahead.

There *is* something life-enhancing and passion-awakening to aim for as we contemplate our elder years. This can be a time of deep fulfillment as we reach the pinnacle of our personal and spiritual growth. Conscious aging is about having meaningful goals for our elderhood that spring from our authentic selves and using the power of intention and inner work to make our vision a reality. It is about having the courage to aim high in an unconscious world.

INTRODUCTION

Leaving behind my journey of struggling and racing through
the white water of many rivers, I become the river,
creating my own unique way.

Leaving behind my self-imposed role as a tree upon
which others have leaned, I now become the wind,
with the freedom to blow whenever and wherever I choose.

Leaving behind the boxes I've created in my life, crammed with
roles, responsibilities, rules and fears,
I become the wild and unpredictable space
within which flowers sprout and grow.

Leaving behind the years of yearning for others
to see me as somebody,
I soften into becoming my future,
with permission from SELF to
continually unfold as I choose, without concern
for how others may see me.

Leaving behind years of telling and teaching,
I become instead a mirror
into which others can peer and
view reflections of themselves to consider.

Leaving behind the urge to provide answers for others,
I become—in the silence of this forest retreat—
the question.

Leaving behind the rigor of my intellect,
I become a single candle in the
darkness, offering myself as a beacon for others
to create their own path.

I become an elder.

by Cathy Carmody

Just as we all take our own paths through life, we approach aging in our own way. We each have our own perception of our (and aging's) limitations and possibilities. I invite you to consider the ways that two friends of mine are approaching their aging—ways that reflect very different expectations, decisions, and understandings—and see how these approaches resonate with you.

Stan eagerly retired from his career in engineering five years ago at the age of fifty-nine, with a good pension and an enviable measure of financial security. He spends his days "puttering around the house" and doing some infrequent volunteer work for a nonprofit in his community. Longevity runs in his family, so Stan feels he may well have three or more decades before him. When I asked him recently about his goals for the upcoming years, he told me that he really doesn't have any—that now it's time to relax, work through his "Honey Do" list, do some traveling, spend time with his children and grandchildren, and bike and play as much racquetball as he can to stay fit, although his aching knees slow him down. He feels he has made his contribution to the world and now it's time for the younger people to step up. When I suggested that he might take a course through a local continuing education program, he laughed and told me that he's done learning. He reiterated that it's time to relax. "Besides, I'm not as sharp as I used to be, so what would be the point?"

Carol, before her retirement from university teaching, took inventory of her talents and interests and reviewed her life. She identified goals that she wanted to realize in the years ahead. She examined her attitudes and fears about aging that could potentially derail her intentions and began to meet with others to explore the possibilities and challenges of this stage of life. Since her retirement, Carol finds deep fulfillment offering workshops in her area of expertise to the community. She also plays a prominent volunteer role in a national educational organization. She is committed to practices that deepen her emotional and spiritual life. She takes courses and attends workshops. She enjoys the rich cultural resources of the city where she lives and makes special dates to take her grandchildren to some of them. She envisions herself contributing to her community for as long as she is physically and mentally able, acknowledging that her contribution may become less visible as the years pass.

Before we go further, I suggest that you take a moment to reflect on these two stories. What feelings did each of them evoke in you? What "Stans" and "Carols" do you know? Which story best reflects how you would like to live as an older adult?

Stan and Carol are approaching their aging in very different ways. Their stories demonstrate the lenses aging is viewed through in contemporary society. These lenses, or paradigms, contrast with one another, but they overlap in many ways. They are in a state of flux as the first tremors of a demographic earthquake shake the cultural landscape. As an estimated ten thousand baby boomers turn sixty-five each day, they do so in an environment characterized by

- Changing economic realities as financial security in retirement becomes more and more elusive and the financial implications of the baby boom generation retiring become a concern to society
- Continual increases in life expectancy and quality of health among older people
- Baby boomers' need to remain engaged and feel relevant
- Increasing recognition of the rich potential of the senior years as a time of profound personal development and contribution to society

As the baby boom generation ages, the proportion of the population over sixty will reach unprecedented heights. This will have an immense impact on every aspect of American life. We need look no further than mainstream media and the internet to find dire predictions of the demographic sea change that is already upon us. Most of these predictions engender alarm about how the retiring baby boomers will drain society's resources. Under the current dominant conception of aging, this may well be true. The ideal held up by the mainstream prescription for aging is retirement (as early as possible), followed by an extended chapter of leisure and disengagement. At the same time, this prescription offers little guidance for how seniors can contribute the skills and wisdom they've acquired over many decades of living and learning.

The baby boom generation—the generation born between 1945 and 1966—has been the vanguard of cultural change since the 1960s. Boomers continually confront entrenched paradigms and cultural prescriptions and have led the way for people-empowering change. As the first waves of this generation hit retirement age, it's easy to imagine how they, or at least that large segment sociologists identify as "cultural creatives," will redefine aging in the coming years. This change is being accomplished on many fronts; it is multi-dimensional, reflecting every aspect of life in the contemporary world. If we think in terms of movements (this energy for change is indeed a culture-changing movement), it is often called the Positive Aging movement. I like to see this emerging paradigm change as a "Positive Aging Rainbow," a multihued set of visions and approaches for older adults to live with more fulfillment, intention, and joy as they age.

Perhaps most visible in this movement is the recognition that lifestyle choices before and during the senior years can make a big difference in the quality of our physical and emotional health. Many of us now know that by combining a healthy lifestyle with the best mainstream and alternative medicine, we can be healthy and active for much longer than our parents or grandparents ever dreamed possible. This approach is often called *healthy aging* or *successful aging*.

Another significant color in this rainbow is the encore movement. With his groundbreaking books *Encore: Finding Work That Matters in the Second Half of Life* and *The Big Shift: Navigating the New Stage Beyond Midlife*, Marc Freedman presents an empowering vision for how retirement can be the doorway to another yet-to-be-named life stage. In this stage people have the opportunity to find or create post-retirement careers in which they do work that matters to them and to society. Such careers can help meet financial needs, provide an opportunity to pursue a deferred dream or passion, or both.

Recognizing the depressing inadequacy of prevailing structures to support housing and the emotional needs of people as they get older, the Aging in Community movement aims to provide workable appealing alternatives to the often depressing, depersonalizing experience of living in a nursing home or similar institution and the isolation and loneliness that often are the hallmark of trying to age in place in one's home. Among the rapidly growing range of alternatives are cohousing communities and various models for "Villages" (based on the Beacon Hill model in Boston), in which members join together to share skills and services, community experiences, and the costs of hiring various providers. A variety of initiatives have been developed to help seniors share services, goods, wisdom, recreation, and most anything else important for human well-being with one another and intergenerationally. The key to all these is *community*, which is so necessary for physical, emotional, and spiritual health throughout life and especially as we age.

Yet another dimension of the Positive Aging movement is the Life Planning movement. This movement encourages older adults to use professionals and strategies to bring intentionality to all facets of their post-retirement lives. This approach recognizes that planning for financial security—the only planning many people do for their senior years—is necessary but insufficient for aging well.

Other facets of this emerging paradigm to empower people as they age include efforts to support older adults in becoming leaders in protecting the earth's environment; programs that support seniors in developing and bringing forth their creativity; and programs such as AARP's Experience Corps and the Senior Corps of the government-sponsored Corporation for National and Community Service, which connects older adults with the people and organizations that need them most.

All these approaches counter the prevailing societal myth that aging is primarily defined by decline, disengagement, and disappointment. They show that such experiences are only a fraction of the larger reality of this life stage. The Positive Aging movement can help many people find greater satisfaction and feel more empowered as they become senior adults. But so much more is possible. The critical contribution of conscious eldering to the Positive Aging movement is recognizing the importance of taking time to focus on inner growth, inner meaning, and purpose. This exploration is the foundation upon which people can most effectively build fulfilling lives. Conscious eldering can empower the other approaches, fostering recognition of the importance of our inner lives as we make decisions about how to live our outer lives. At the same time, this inner work helps temper the denial of aging and mortality that can easily be the dark side of many of the new approaches to aging. It enables us to grow and thrive emotionally and spiritually as we inherit the legacy our lives have prepared us for.

Frequently, people nearing "normal" retirement age tell me that this new vision of aging sounds unrealistic. In this difficult economic environment, many people are not financially able to retire. They see positive aging and conscious eldering as luxuries for the well-off, who have time and money to invest in creative inner and outer exploration. I firmly believe that this does not need to be the case, as you will see throughout this book. Aging positively and consciously is about believing in our potential for fulfillment, growth, and service. It is not dependent on our life circumstances or our financial situation. The consciousness and intention we bring to our lives as we age are much more important than the material forms they take.

In addition to changing the way we deal with aging, it is critically important to change the words we associate with growing older. I have met many people, including those who come to our Choosing Conscious Elderhood retreats, who feel a call to meaning as they age. They sense that there is some role for them that is different than just being a "senior" or "older adult" or "elderly." But they usually have little if any idea of what this status would look like, how to get there, or even the vocabulary to describe and name it.

In most indigenous cultures, there is a designated, revered, and empowering role for elders, along with a set of cultural expectations for how elders develop their wisdom and then serve the community in that role. (When I refer to indigenous peoples, I am employing a term commonly used by anthropologists to refer to cultures that are or were able to live their traditional, close-to-the-earth lifestyles in a way not heavily impacted by the values of the industrial, commercially oriented world.) Most of the world's people today, whether Eastern or Western, do not live in such an indigenous society; we live in a modern world that has gained much in terms of material comfort and security but one that has also lost a great deal of understanding of what it means to live attuned with the natural world.

In our world, the word *elder* is equated with frailty, being over the hill, past the stage of significantly contributing to the community, living in recreation-oriented gated communities if one can afford it, and being a drain on the country's resources. It's understandable that many older people, especially those who are still healthy and active, do not want to be identified by the term *elder*. It is no wonder Elderhostel recently changed its name to the less age-specific Road Scholar. The term *senior* is preferable for many, but given the lack of a meaningful role for older adults, even this term carries a lot of disempowering baggage. Why else would cosmetic surgery and Botox be such booming businesses? Why else are so many of us hesitant to reveal our age? No one wants to be seen as old.

However, as awareness grows, more people are learning that the often disempowering term *elder* has the potential to reflect something vastly different: a level of growth and service that is critical to the well-being of the community. Conscious aging can mean more than just becoming a bit more conscious as we age. For many, that alone does not satisfy the need to have a meaningful role in the community and a larger sense of personal identity. An inspiring vision of what is possible is that of becoming a *conscious elder*. Rather than feeding a pervasive denial of aging, the term *elder* can instead connote the fulfillment of the human yearning for meaning, growth, and service in life's later chapters.

The role of the elder is archetypal. It's deeply embedded in the human psyche and has been expressed in the world's cultures, up until the modern industrial and post-industrial era. The wisdom and gifts of elders have been universally valued as necessary for the emotional and spiritual health and balance of societies. This archetypal energy still seeks expression today amid the many powerful changes shaking the cultural landscape. In indigenous cultures, the role of elder was clearly defined; in today's highly diverse world, the expressions of this energy—the forms modern elderhood will take—will be as diverse as modern culture. And they will be different for people in early elderhood (young elders) than for those in their later elderhood. The challenge of defining and embodying this role in today's world is daunting but has immense possibilities for enriching the lives of older people as society benefits from their skills and wisdom.

We do not become elders in the sense this book encourages and supports by merely *wanting* to do so. The journey toward elderhood requires conscious effort and preparation. Throughout this book, the word *conscious* is the key. *Conscious eldering, conscious aging*, and *spiritual eldering* are frequently used terms that generally refer to the same inner process. They all refer to a commitment to bringing as high a level of awareness and intentionality as possible to every facet of our lives as we age. I prefer to use the term *conscious eldering* because it makes explicit the fact that such work can aim high toward a goal—becoming an elder—with rich and empowering possibilities.

Conscious eldering means being intentional in all our decisions, rather than acting out of habit or societal programming. It requires working to get in touch with our deepest yearnings for our elder years and creating a lifestyle that supports our personal fulfillment. It involves strengthening our connection with the spiritual dimension of ourselves, where our passions and callings flow from. And it means that we work to transform our inner blockages—beliefs, attitudes, unhealed wounds, unexamined life experiences—that impede that flow.

The approaches to the inner work of conscious eldering presented in this book draw heavily from four sources:

- The universally recognized dynamics of the life transition process and the rites of passage that mark major transition
- The wisdom of Rabbi Zalman Schachter-Shalomi, who, along with Ram Dass and others, taught the first conscious aging courses at Omega Institute some twenty years ago, and who wrote the seminal work on conscious aging, *From Age-ing to Sage-ing*

- My own journey along the path of conscious eldering
- Perhaps most important of all, what I have learned from the courageous, committed elders and elders-in-the-making who have brought their fears and visions, sorrows and joys, confusions and commitments to the workshops and Choosing Conscious Elderhood retreats

Rites of Passage, Nature, and Conscious Eldering

The way our psyche changes as we shift from midlife adulthood to early elderhood is reflected in traditional rites of passage around the world. This book's chapters mirror the three-phase template for virtually all significant inner transformations as well as structured rites of passage. It is also a powerful framework for you to understand and structure your own inner work. Our retreats are structured as rites of passage; this book sequentially follows the major themes of these rites to help you navigate your own transition into a conscious elderhood.

In these modern times, most of us spend the majority of our time in man-made environments, removed from the natural world. There is a reason why most traditional rites of passage required people to leave their villages and spend time alone in the natural world. Likewise, large portions of our retreats involve time in nature. The natural world has the power to open hearts and minds and help us experience what is authentic in ourselves. Our authentic self, our spiritual dimension, is the source of our deepest and truest passion, vision, and calling to serve the world. Tapping the power of nature can be tremendously beneficial for you as you move through your passage into conscious elderhood.

How Best to Gain Value from This Book

This book is not another academic work. Instead, it is a guidebook to support your journey toward conscious elderhood. You will learn conscious eldering practices and their rationale, be inspired by stories from retreat participants who have benefited from these practices, and learn empowering rituals that you can adapt to meet your own needs.

As you begin this book and whenever you pick it up to continue your reading, I offer these suggestions: Approach this book slowly and consciously. Allow it to lead you into an inner exploration instead of being merely another book of growth concepts that inspires you for the moment and then ends up on a shelf as you move on to your next reading. Many of us have the misconception that having information is equated with growth. In contrast, my lifetime of commitment to my own growth and that of others has shown me that growth and the attainment of wisdom are the result of information reflected and acted upon. Many books can make us feel good for a while, as they give us a sense of what might be possible. However, a book will only affect your life if it motivates you to take action in your inner and outer worlds. I hope this book can make a positive difference for you.

I recommend that you create a tranquil context for yourself as you work with this book. It will help you align with the energy I am bringing to it. Each time you work with a chapter (I suggest you work with only one chapter on a given day), imagine yourself in a peaceful retreat center surrounded by magnificent natural beauty. You are with a group of ten to twelve people, aged fifty-five to eighty, and two guides. Like you, they are all seeking to age consciously. They share a strong commitment to living with passion, purpose, and intention as they age. This group continually invokes the presence of the Great Mystery (which they know by many different names) to open their minds and touch their hearts.

In this group, your ongoing experience is one of being held and supported by a loving, safe community. Here you can feel safe speaking what is true for you. Here you can experience the synergy that enables you and each of the others to do deeper inner work than you could likely do on your own. This may be the only place in your life where you can be with others like you—ones who seek to understand what conscious elderhood can mean for them. By envisioning such support as you read, you may be laying the inner groundwork for creating or finding the community support that is critical for conscious eldering.

Each chapter ends with a Story by the Fire. Imagine your group sitting around a fire, engaging in the most powerful learning activity known to humankind throughout the ages: telling stories of experience and growth. These stories, each written by someone who has been deeply impacted by the conscious eldering practice, are filled with passion and heart. Read them slowly and savor them. Imagine hearing them spoken with the sounds of the crackling fire in the background. See what they evoke in you. Do you recognize your own story in their words? If you don't hear it at first, you may later as you do the inner work of conscious eldering.

As you read and work with this guidebook, be aware that others will be doing the same. You are not alone. Many others hear the call to aim high and age consciously. In addition to using this book, you can access other excellent resources, some of which can be found at the end of this book. Increasing numbers of people participate in conscious eldering retreats, workshops, webinars, elder wisdom circles, and conscious aging discussion groups throughout the world. In

recent years, a growing body of research has demonstrated the power
of shared intention to create energy fields that can raise the consciousness of all involved and even impact the larger culture. I encourage
you to use the power of your intention to align with others seeking to
grow into a *conscious* elderhood. Together, we will learn to age consciously and make this a more conscious world.

Let's begin this exploration. The world needs conscious elders.

1

CONSCIOUS ELDERING:
THE JOURNEY TO WHOLENESS
AS WE AGE

It's all about perspective. The mouse's narrow, up-close perspective of the world is very different than the broad view of the eagle. The perspective of our ego is very different than that of our spiritual dimension. Mouse and eagle—personality and soul—live together with different types of awareness.

Our egos view our experiences, our goals, and our beliefs about fulfillment through a lens that is shaped and colored by our society. Our spiritual dimension, which has many names (I prefer to call it our soul) sees a purpose for our lives that is not conditioned by cultural norms and values.*

---

* In referring to the spark of the divine within each of us—the essence of our individuality at the deepest level—I use the word *soul*. If this usage doesn't resonate with you, substitute whatever term you find most meaningful. In describing the ineffable wisdom and energy that is the source and essence of all life, I prefer the name *the Great Mystery*. Again, use whatever term is most meaningful for you.

How we perceive our lives and the reality of our aging depends upon the depth and breadth of our view of life's purpose. Of course, we all have egos; they are the vehicles that enable us to function in a material world. In many ways, the viewpoints and values of our culture are necessary for the development of healthy, effective egos. Our soul, however, is what gives us the ability to access a higher consciousness that is aware of the big picture. Our soul has the wisdom and energy to help us learn from experiences and create those that can assist us in fulfilling the greater purpose of our lives. We have both mouse and eagle in us. Both parts are integral to who we are, and recognizing this is key to understanding conscious eldering.

Conscious Eldering's Role in the New Vision

In the introduction, we examined a new paradigm of how aging is viewed in contemporary society. All its facets help empower us as we age, replacing a sense of diminishment, lack of purpose, and dearth of opportunity with a much brighter vision for our elder chapters. The Positive Aging movement is emerging and growing at a time when medical advances are making possible longer lives with more years of good health and the ability to be physically active. This momentous shift will result in a great many older people finding a measure of happiness and life satisfaction that was not imaginable until the last couple of decades or so. However, for many, even this is not enough.

What is lacking from most of the approaches of the Positive Aging movement is recognition of the spiritual dimension of aging—the soul's eye view of our human life cycle. For a great many baby boomers, the primary value of these Positive Aging approaches is that they can help us extend the stage of midlife adulthood or add a second stage of midlife adulthood until we reach the stage of very old age. At the point when even "age-defying" and "age-reversing" diets, supplements, and lifestyle choices can no longer defy our mortality, we are on our own to prepare for death. Without considering the spiritual dimension, these approaches reinforce the glorification of youth and the denial of mortality and aging. With this denial comes devaluation of the aging process. A primary understanding of the dynamics of the human psyche is lost, and with it precious opportunity for growth and service in life's elder chapters. I am not suggesting that the Positive Aging movement is not valuable. It's certainly making a beneficial difference. I am saying that the inner work of conscious eldering is essential for bringing wholeness to this emerging vision of aging and to those who seek to be all they can be as they age.

Elderhood As a Life Stage

To understand conscious elderhood, it is important to recognize that the psyche moves through stages throughout our lives. Each stage presents opportunities for growth and challenges. If we try to hold on to any stage or get stuck, our opportunities for experiencing the fullness of the next stage's potential—all the growth, service, and satisfaction it offers—will be severely limited. At the same time, our experience in our current stage may become stale and unsatisfying, as our energies are not flowing freely in the direction they want to move in. In relation to aging, Carl Jung, the preeminent researcher of the human psyche, characterized this reality in this oft-quoted passage: "Wholly unprepared we take the step into the afternoon of life. Worse still, we take this step with the false presupposition that our truths and ideals will serve us as hitherto. But we cannot live the afternoon of life according to the program of life's morning—for what was great in the morning will be little at evening, and what in the morning was true will at evening have become a lie."[1]

With today's extended lifespans, it may well be the case that the afternoon of our lives begins later than it did in Jung's time. There is not much value in debating whether it begins at sixty or sixty-five or seventy or later. What is important is to recognize that something begins to shift for most people as they begin to approach retirement age and envision life beyond. Those attuned to the needs of their psyches and promptings of their souls are aware of this shift; those not so attuned may not be aware. In either case, it is happening. There is a subtle inner call to introspection and less focus on outer activity. This call includes a tendency to spend time looking back on life experiences and trying to make sense of them. It brings into our awareness the subject of legacy—the legacy we have created so far and the legacy we have the potential to manifest as elders. And even with its modern association with being old and frail, something about the word *elder* resonates in many of us. It is some archetypal memory of a role in the human family that is important, valued, and honored.

The term *conscious eldering* implies and describes recognition of, preparation for, and movement toward the role of elder. We do not live in a society where this role is established and supported. Our modern world, where a much higher proportion of the population lives into old age and secular values dominate the collective consciousness, is vastly different. However, the role of elder is archetypal, built into the human psyche over countless generations. That energy is alive in us. That role remains as necessary as ever for the collective human race and for the individual's wholeness and fulfillment in life's afternoon and evening. The ways conscious elders will fill that role in today's world will be as diverse as modern society; it is as true now as it was in the indigenous world that this role requires preparation—conscious preparation. This process is the essence of conscious eldering.

The word *conscious* is key to understanding our potential for growth and wholeness as we age and the range of practices that can help move us toward realizing our potential. There is a distinction between merely growing old and growing into elderhood. Becoming conscious means becoming increasingly aware—aware of who we are at the most authentic level of ourselves; aware of the part of ourselves that is conditioned by the many often disempowering messages implanted by society and family; aware of our emotions and how they operate in us; aware of our talents, passions, aspirations, and deepest callings; aware of our strengths and weaknesses; aware of attitudes, beliefs, habits, and shadow elements that disempower us, block our radiance, and sabotage our potential. Becoming conscious means becoming aware of the emotional baggage and encumbrances we are carrying as we move beyond midlife adulthood, such as unhealed wounds, unfelt and unprocessed grief, grudges and heart-closing attitudes that require forgiveness, and stories of unworthiness or victimhood we have constructed over decades to define our lives. Becoming conscious means increasing our ability to see our lives with an eagle's-eye view. As we do this work, we embark on a growth process guided by our soul, which is working to unfold in our lives through all our experiences, whether we perceive them as positive or negative.

From an even broader perspective, growing in consciousness means growing in awareness (experientially as well as conceptually) of our connectedness. We are one with all of humanity and with the living planet that supports a vast web of interdependence. This is where, as theologian Frederick Buechner described, "our deepest gladness and the world's hunger meet."[2] From that knowing, we can make our most fulfilling and important contributions as elders. And at yet another level—higher consciousness—lies the experience of the Great Mystery itself, the source and essence of all.

The work of conscious eldering is grounded in increasing our awareness and then acting on what we know. The more conscious we become, the more whole we are. However, this work is not easy. It requires commitment, perseverance, and support. It is counteracted on every level by the heavy, dark cloud of unconsciousness we all live in. Perhaps that is why classical descriptions of experiences with higher consciousness are so often filled with brilliant light. After even small breakthroughs in awareness, we feel a wonderful sense of "lightness." The opposite of being conscious is operating automatically. With the ever-escalating pace of the modern, multitasking life, it is not easy to allow ourselves to slow down. When we shift out of autopilot, we can let consciousness shine through, accompanied by awareness and intentional action.

This work may seem daunting—a challenge reserved for only the most evolved or gifted people. You may conclude that you are not one of those special few; you may not feel worthy or capable of such wholeness. You may think you don't have the time and resources to prepare for such an elderhood. Lest you despair, the good news is that we don't need to completely fulfill any ideal of conscious elderhood to allow our potential elder wisdom and gifts to be recognized. Everything we can give brings us great fulfillment; in small or large ways, we are helping to heal our world. Every bit of inner work we do frees up energy and helps our light shine brighter.

Before we delve into what conscious eldering can be in today's world, let's look at the archetypal role of elder. Throughout human history, elders have been nurturers of community, spiritual leaders, guardians of traditions, and teachers. They have been the storytellers.

They have helped the younger generations inherit the enduring wisdom and deeper meanings of life that lie beneath the surface. In his book *Nature and the Human Soul*, Bill Plotkin summarizes the role of elders by noting that they have traditionally contributed to the human and more-than-human communities by:

- Defending and nurturing the innocence and wonder of children
- Mentoring and initiating adolescents
- Mentoring adults in their soulwork
- Guiding cultural evolution or transformation
- Maintaining the balance between human culture and the larger earth community[3]

In his book *Fruitful Aging: Finding the Gold In the Golden Years*, Tom Pinkson lists several ways the elder archetype has manifested in the lives of conscious elders in both the past and present. These manifestations are unique to each person's personality. They may take the form of an artist or a teacher, a contemplative or a healer, a builder or explorer, or any number of others. The most important thing is to remember that "all these archetypes of the Wisdom Elder live in the inner depths, so going deep within to nurture their growth is a necessity."[4]

Until modern times, the role of an elder was highly respected. The well-being of the society depended upon the wisdom and wholeness of its elders. While people who lived to ripe old age were relatively rare and accorded deep respect, partly because survival itself required strength, intelligence, and adaptability, not everyone with gray hair and a wrinkled face was recognized as a leader among the people. In these close-knit communities, people lived together all their lives and knew each other's gifts and weaknesses. They recognized those with the potential to serve in the elder role and nurtured this potential so that their culture would have the elders it needed.

The changing views of society have resulted in a general shift away from the traditional reverence of the elder role. Because of this, it is rarely seen outside of more indigenous cultures, like that of the Rarámuri (more commonly known as Tarahumara) of Copper Canyon, Mexico, who place great importance on the elder role of Mayori, which roughly translates as "person of wisdom." These are the indigenous people I am most familiar with. I have had two opportunities in recent years to colead conscious eldering pilgrimages to Copper Canyon in northern Mexico with Jan Milburn and his Rarámuri wife, Mireya Ayala. Jan, founder of the Milburn Foundation International, has spent the past forty years as a tireless champion of the Rarámuri, living continuously for fifteen years with them as he has fought to preserve their magnificent land and indigenous culture from the relentless onslaught of Western values and lifestyle. Anthropologists consider the Rarámuri (a population of seventy thousand strong, spread throughout several Grand Canyon–sized canyons collectively known as Barranca del Cobre or Copper Canyon) to be one of the Native American cultures least changed by Western culture. Jan's mission has been to help preserve core elements of the Rarámuri way of life, which is deeply grounded in sustainability, while helping modern society recognize the value of indigenous wisdom.

In recognition of his wisdom and deep spirituality, Jan was invited to undergo Mayori training by the leaders in the area of Copper Canyon, where he was active and most known. He was the only white man ever to be initiated into this role. Mayori is the fullest expression of eldering. Although Mayori is traditionally a male role, the wives of Mayori receive extensive informal training and are often as influential, though unofficially, as their husbands. The process of becoming a Mayori typically lasts twelve years and consists of four three-year cycles of learning. A Mayori-in-training studies physical, emotional, and spiritual healing with shamans, herbal healers, and other Mayori. He eventually becomes the community member with the most in-depth knowledge of the traditions and values of the tribe. He is trained as a mediator and is well versed in psychology and the workings of the human psyche and personality; he can bring balance and insight when the people turn to him to help them resolve conflict.

Spiritual training is perhaps the most critical component of Mayori preparation. A Mayori's role includes assuring that the ceremonies, rituals, dances, and initiations that sustain the emotional and spiritual lives of the community are taught and conducted properly. He is the one the people turn to for his deep insight and awareness of the larger picture when they are confronted with new challenges. For example, the Mayori took the lead in helping the Rarámuri find a way to employ Christian practices introduced by the Spaniards in support of their traditional spirituality; this compromise appeased the missionaries while honoring Rarámuri spiritual beliefs. Among indigenous people living in harsh conditions, living in balance with each other and the natural world is absolutely critical to survival. Mayori elders play the role of guiding the Rarámuri to maintain this balance. To do this, the elders must first attain wholeness within themselves so that using the power of their inner wholeness, they can work to keep the culture and their environment intact.

Of course, we live in a different world than the Rarámuri. It would not be possible or even desirable to try to re-create the role of the Mayori or its equivalent in our society. However, the role of elder, so deeply embedded in the human psyche, is still urgently needed in our perilous times. The gifts and wisdom of conscious elders are critical for restoring our world with balance, seasoned experience, wholeness, and an understanding of interrelationship. These elements are necessary for the cultural transformation that can assure a future for our descendants and our planet's ecosystems. Our challenge today is creatively defining this role and according it the honor and respect it deserves. This redefinition is a work in progress, as are those of us feeling called to elderhood; we make conscious, intentional efforts to grow so that our elder gifts can naturally flow.

In contemporary society, as in indigenous cultures, conscious elders share their gifts and wisdom. They also nurture their inner lives, cultivating their spiritual and psychological growth. The focus of most younger elders (those in early elderhood) tends to be weighted toward outer activity that expresses their gifts. This expression is attuned to the soul's guidance, rather than driven by the ego. Those in later elderhood, with their energy levels waning and awareness of mortality ever more present, become more focused on their inner lives. Conscious elders I have known who are in their later elderhood serve the community less through visible projects or activities than through their relationships. They radiate the compassion, peace, wisdom, and joy that emerge as their souls shine—the result of their commitment to inner growth. People of all ages are attracted to their radiance.

The inner work that I present in this book is vitally important for elders at any point on the continuum of elderhood. For those in or approaching early elderhood, this work heals life's wounds, releases old baggage, develops spiritual connection, and nurtures the vision, passion, and sense of purpose that are all necessary for serving as true elders in the community. For those in later elderhood, whose outer lives may have become "simpler," this ongoing inner work can create the sense of fulfillment that comes from approaching the pinnacle of their potential for psychological and spiritual growth. This work also prepares them for their life's final transition so that they may leave this life peacefully and cross the threshold with an unburdened soul.

I Still Feel Young. Why Not Wait Until Later?

Many people seeking a fulfilling alternative to the mainstream paradigm for aging feel they can dedicate themselves to conscious aging work when they become really old. They want to wait until they must finally stop identifying as a midlife adult; they say there's no point in focusing on elderhood while they are still active and feeling vibrant. There are consequential flaws with this reasoning.

For most of us, finding our deepest passions and callings and removing the blocks to their full expression takes a lot of focus, work, and time. This isn't accomplished at a retreat or weekend workshop or by reading a few books, although all these can give us a glimpse of what is possible. Psychology and the emerging field of neuropsychology verify what we know intuitively—that changing habitual behaviors and attitudes, whatever our age, is very difficult. To borrow from an old adage, when the going gets tough, you get what you practice.

As we age, the mental energy that fuels this inner work often dwindles, especially if we are aging with a lot of baggage. As a result, by the time we think we're old enough to begin, the juice for doing the work may be gone. On the other hand, if we start this inner work during the years of our early elderhood (in our late fifties and early sixties), we may well be able to gain more satisfaction and contribute more to the greater good than if we wait until we are very old, have less energy, and are naturally more inwardly focused.

Committing to prepare for conscious elderhood before or soon after we reach retirement age can also free us from the disempowering denial of aging. By doing this, we can counteract forces that suppress our ability to fulfill our potential as we age.

Perhaps more important than the personal benefits of engaging in conscious eldering work now rather than waiting until later is how our work can benefit the world we live in. These are times of crisis. The world teeters on a knife edge between cultural and ecological collapse and cultural transformation. Our world cannot afford to have tens of millions of its citizens (many highly educated and skilled) believing that they are incapable of making a difference in their elder years. The world needs conscious elders who shine as beacons of hope in the darkness of fear, elders championing and modeling life-sustaining values and using their wisdom and compassion to heal a wounded planet.

STORY BY THE FIRE
Living As a Candle in the Darkness
by Cathy Carmody

After a long management career in large organizations, I chose to take early retirement in 1995 and move on to create a business partnership to deliver leadership and personal development programs. Ten years after that, I published a book reflecting on my lifetime of inner discoveries. I then went on to form a company involved in supporting individuals, especially women, in the evolution of their consciousness—work that I felt very passionate about.

In 2010 I let it all fall away. I had managed to exhaust myself in my efforts to support others. I finally woke up to the reality that I had wanted more for them than they wanted for themselves. Ironically, while I encouraged others to listen to the messages from their inner selves, I had ignored my own inner knowing that I was pushing myself over the edge.

I spent the years from mid-2010 to early 2012 in various states of chaos. I alternated between relishing days of quietness to doing bits of the same consulting work to railing at myself for not knowing what else to do. I slowly came to realize that I was done with my old work and midlife career. At the same time, I knew with deep certainty that I had much more to contribute to the world, and a life of decline and diminishment was definitely not what I wanted. More than anything, I wanted—and intended—to have a life full of purpose and deep meaning. What I didn't know was the form this would take.

Gradually, clarity began to emerge. At first, it wasn't about words; it was more a "knowing" I felt in my body. I found myself paying close attention to what felt important to me and how that feeling moved through the tissues in my body. I began to gain a sense that my future work would not be as separate from my past work as I had originally thought, yet I knew it would be very different. I had a strong feeling that my work around consciousness would continue, but this time it would flow from my ongoing curiosity and discoveries about my aging process. I realized that I wanted to age consciously, rather than as dictated by the myths that surrounded aging. One of my memories that surfaced around this time contained an image of an older woman walking past me on a street. I remembered that when it happened, I felt a deep sense of wanting to be her. I felt envious of her; she had something very precious that I wanted. I wasn't sure what this memory meant at the time, but I had a feeling that it was significant and would eventually become clear.

As the months unfolded, I came to recognize that my beliefs and expectations, rather than my biological limitations, were the greatest challenge. I also came to believe that by consciously shifting any negative and limiting beliefs I had about growing older, I could open the door to an incredibly powerful scenario for aging that would allow me to manifest a whole new way of being for the next years of my life.

Finally, in the summer of 2012 I responded to the call I had first heard several years before. I attended a Choosing Conscious Elderhood retreat. From the minute I stepped off the plane in Vancouver to the minute I left the Sea to Sky Retreat Centre one week later, I knew I was exactly in the right place. My sense of uncertainty left me, and while I didn't have all the answers, I came to know with a level of sureness that I was on my new path. By the time I left the retreat, I believed strongly that conscious elders would lead the new vision of aging into the future; if I chose to, I could be one of those elders.

On the second to last day of the retreat, after many hours of sitting quietly with only the trees, the sky, wind, and birds to keep me company, I wrote a poem titled "Becoming an Elder." I was surprised by what I wrote. It left me wondering what else I had to say that I hadn't given myself permission to voice. What else could I leave behind that would clear my path ahead? It confirmed my commitment to being a mirror, a single candle, and a beacon for the emergence of conscious aging. I left the retreat with a strong intention to manifest what I had written and become a voice for conscious aging.

I now know what my memory long ago featuring the older woman was all about. She was a forerunner of my future self and the life I am now beginning to experience. Everything is beginning to come together. My life is flowing into a place where I can choose to live my life totally my way, rather than as a reflection of someone else's idea of how I should live. It is a time of revelations about who I

*Cathy's poem opens the introduction to this book.

have the potential to become, without need for apologies to anyone or paying heed to any myths around aging. It is a time for harvesting the wisdom from my years and sharing what is meaningful with others. It's a time of deep satisfaction and joy. The life I am growing into was what I envied about the older woman; this was what I felt and now know is so precious. A life fleetingly sensed long ago, described in my poetry, and created day by day by my conscious choices. A life lived as a candle in the darkness.

2

LIFE TRANSITIONS AND RITES OF PASSAGE: PORTALS TO CONSCIOUS ELDERHOOD

Ten mature adults and two guides, each engaged in silent prayer and accompanied by a gentle drumbeat, stand on the edge of a mesa at Ghost Ranch, New Mexico. The chill of a late-springtime dawn at seven thousand feet is dispelled as the sun rises over sandstone monoliths and pinnacles to the east. Sunlight gradually envelops the mesa, illuminating the new tender green of the scrub oak and cottonwoods as they emerge from a long, cold winter. The call of a golden eagle soaring overhead pierces the silence. It summons the world to life and to revel in this new day. To the west, the walls that enclose this natural amphitheater are appearing from darkness to reveal a stunning palette of layered color ranging from white-gray to beige to vermillion. It is the season of new beginnings for a group of people enacting rites of passage to inform and empower their journeys into conscious elderhood.

These individuals, in or approaching their elder years, are participating in a Choosing Conscious Elderhood retreat. They are following in the footsteps of countless others. At critical turning points in life, people have retreated to wilderness places to enact rites of passage. They then returned to their communities spiritually and emotionally renewed, with new insight about how best to live and contribute as the next stages of their lives unfolded.

Anthropologists tell us that throughout most of known human history, many cultures marked significant life changes with rites of passage that served as initiation into the next stage of life. Extensive preparation at all levels—physical, psychological, and spiritual— was followed by an intense, spiritually charged ceremonial ritual process. This ceremony required the initiate to leave behind normal village life and enter a place of mystery, perceived danger, and spiritual power. The intent of this process was to acknowledge that a major life transition was occurring, both inwardly and outwardly, and to empower the initiate to fully and consciously move into his next life role.

Through these powerful processes, people were assisted in letting go of attitudes, behaviors, and self-concepts from previous life stages that would not serve them or their communities in their new role. Concurrently, they were guided in identifying and strengthening the skills, wisdom, psychological resources, and spiritual connection necessary for claiming their new status and fulfilling their new roles. Upon their return to the community, they and their communities knew that in some essential way who they had been—both personally and in terms of their role in society—had died. A new self with new wisdom and gifts to contribute had been born.

Our secular contemporary world is characterized by a dearth of meaningful, emotionally and spiritually empowering rites of passage to help people realize the potential fullness of each of life's stages. Deep wisdom about human growth has been lost. As they pass through life, people are expected to move from one ill-defined stage to another alone, with little psychological and spiritual preparation. The two areas where this lack is most detrimental to personal and societal well-being are the ambiguous passage from adolescence into adulthood and the equally amorphous passage from career-focused adulthood into early elderhood.

In their chapter "Transition from Childhood to Adolescence" in the excellent anthology on rites of passage, past and present, *Betwixt and Between: Patterns of Masculine and Feminine Initiation*, John Allan and Pat Dyke wrote that in many ways our present Western civilization is an exception in human history because of its lack of emotionally and spiritually empowering rites of passage into young adulthood. They note that Western civilization has not completely abandoned such rites, which still exist in the form of bar and bat mitzvah, confirmation, graduation, and marriage, but Allan and Dyke also acknowledge that to have such rites reduced to this level "is unusual, for in other cultures the rites of passage involved all levels of community, from the elders who steered the process to the very young who joined in the celebrations."[1] But by and large, most young people today are left to make or discover their own challenges or rites of initiation, and in many cases such misguided attempts are destructive rather than life affirming. While they do mark changes in external life status, graduation and marriage for most people do not provide the preparation and challenge to support the inner development that is the purpose of true rites of passage. And in today's world, religion-based rites usually involve much more memorization of sacred texts and beliefs than the deep self-examination and the psychological challenge necessary to encounter the limits of who they have been and to discover the emotional and spiritual strength their growth requires.

However, because of their critical importance for human growth and well-being, it is inevitable that empowering rites of passage into adulthood will again emerge. This is already beginning to happen. In the past few decades, several organizations, such as the School of Lost Borders and Rite of Passage Journeys, have begun offering programs for teens on the threshold of adulthood that incorporate the elements identified by anthropologists as inherent to all indigenous rites of passage. On a larger scale, programs like Outward Bound and other outdoor challenge-focused organizations have served as de facto rites of passage for many young people, although these programs don't directly address the spiritual dimension of this critical life transition.

Looking at the other end of life, with the exception of a few individuals, organizations, and men's and women's groups working to develop meaningful ceremonies and educational programs to support people making the passage into elderhood, there is little awareness of the value of such processes for those seeking to grow into the undefined and largely unsupported role of elder. In fact, there is little awareness of the reality that true elderhood is the product of an inner passage that must be navigated with or without the support of structured rite of passage ceremonies supported and witnessed by one's community.

However, even though most Western cultures ignore the importance of such rites of passage, there are others who understand why marking these milestones is crucial to our spiritual and emotional health. Indigenous peoples recognize, as do many contemporary life-cycle development theorists, that optimal human development occurs in discrete stages. These are stages of inner development that, in today's world, may or may not coincide with the roles we play in the outer world. The inner and outer dynamics of each life stage must be recognized and supported for the person to flourish and make her full contribution. If the psychological tasks and potentials of each stage are not supported, development may well be hindered or aborted. Lack of cultural recognition and support for this process is why many people with adult bodies and roles never grow out of childhood or adolescence on an emotional level. It is also why many people with aging bodies continue to try to live as though they are forty or fifty, often as parodies of their midlife selves, never actualizing or even being aware of the rich possibilities of aging and of the necessary inner work that prepares one for the passage into the stage of conscious elderhood.

Rites of passage exist to recognize that we do not fulfill the potential of life's developmental stages by just gradually drifting through our lifespan. At certain key times, the human psyche needs some significant experience that has the potential to catapult us from the security of our current stage to a journey toward the unknown potential and the next chapter. Some people are able to use such catalysts (whether consciously or not, with or without support) to serve as de facto rites of passage in their inner development. Many others, with little or no awareness of the call to growth and few tools to respond to it, are not able to do so.

Formal rites of passage were developed to provide structured ways of supporting what the psyche attempts to accomplish as we humans move through life's stages. Their purpose is to emphasize the significance of the inner and outer transitions the initiates are undergoing. They help dismantle those elements of previous life stages that will not promote growth and wholeness in the next. They force a descent into the depths of oneself to courageously encounter disempowering (and usually unconscious) habits, attitudes, beliefs, and emotional blockages (what psychologists call "the shadow") as well as unrecognized strength and potential. Such rites provide the opportunity for a life-transforming experience of one's spiritual and emotional resources and for receiving the vision and empowerment that come with embracing this metamorphosis.

Psychologists and others who study human development tell us that all significant life transitions, in order to successfully realize their potential, consist of a three-phase process. Its duration depends upon the individual's unique psychological makeup, the external circumstances of his life, and the amount of support he gets during the transition. This three-phase process begins with separation from the life we have lived, progresses to an in-between phase where we are no longer quite who we have been but are not yet who we can become, and ends with fully moving into new beginnings.

Likewise, anthropologists who have studied the many forms that formal, community-sanctioned rites of passage have taken around the world tell us that they are all characterized by this same three-phase process. These rites unfold over a period of weeks or months and are punctuated by a shorter, highly focused ritual process that encapsulates and intensifies this three-phase dynamic. These rites are still practiced in various indigenous societies that are striving to hold on to their wisdom about human growth in this secular, modern world. Several of the contributions in *Betwixt and Between* point out that the relatively few (but increasing) adaptations of these rites to meet the needs of people living in contemporary society draw upon the power of this same three-phase process.[2]

Whether supported by a formal rite of passage process or not, the inner work to respond to the psyche's call to growth must be successfully accomplished in order for human beings to grow from one life stage to the next. The extent to which we accomplish these tasks has much to do with how we move from who we have been to who we have the potential to become. Our work is to leave behind what will not serve us in life's next stage; to carry forward those qualities and gifts that will serve us well; and to discover and embody new gifts and potentials that expand our ability to find fulfillment, while serving the greater community in our new life roles.

If this inner work of transition is not accomplished, our growth is slowed and our potential is not fulfilled. All life, human and other-than-human, requires endings and beginnings in order to thrive. If we humans remain stuck in a life stage, a life that may have previously seemed fulfilling loses its zest and we stagnate. Our efforts to experience aliveness may become increasingly futile, dysfunctional, and desperate. We lose connection with any vision of who we can become, beyond who we have been or are now. Hope becomes replaced by resignation, aliveness by numbness, growth by stagnation, and authenticity by conformity.

Despite the importance of this inner work of transition, I can find few examples in anthropological literature of rites of passage to initiate elders. In societies such as the Rarámuri of Copper Canyon, certain people are groomed for and initiated into special elder roles that are easily recognizable by the outside world. However, we don't hear much about formal rites of passage into elderhood. I believe this is because the indigenous wisdom of traditional societies recognized the critical importance of elders and supported the development of elder gifts and wisdom in an ongoing way as people aged. Training for the role of elder was embedded in the social fabric. As people aged, they were expected to learn the values and traditions of the community, develop a strong connection with the world of the sacred, work toward personal wholeness, and prepare to serve as mentors to the younger generations. Due to shorter life expectancy, elder was a life stage that relatively few people entered, and among these, some were more capable of and prepared to embody elder wisdom than others.

Our contemporary world differs greatly from that of indigenous cultures. For them, truly empowering growth-supporting processes were (and, in a rapidly decreasing number of cultures, still are) intrinsic to their way of life. For the first time in human history, the majority of people live long enough to have the opportunity to enter elderhood. The reality of attaining old age is a much less special and less honored accomplishment. Specialists now fill many of the roles that were historically filled by elders. We have largely lost an understanding of the dynamics of life transition, so elderhood—as a developmental stage and a societal role—is a dynamic that modern culture is only beginning to understand and define. However, we have the same needs as our ancestors. For those who feel called to the elder role, the inner work to transition from midlife adulthood to elderhood with awareness, intention, and commitment is critical. Formal rites of passage, which may take many forms, can in today's world play a key role in empowering people to do this inner work and acknowledge, for themselves and those dear to them, that they are indeed claiming the role of elder.

While the call to elderhood may gradually enter our awareness as we move through adulthood, many will hear it more dramatically. In today's world, many of us have lost our sensitivity to the promptings of our psyches. Our awareness of the call may well be precipitated by an external event and resultant sense of crisis. It may take the form of loss of employment, death of a dream, ending of a relationship, diminishment of health or abilities, retirement, or any number of other major life events. Or, if we don't have such an external crisis, we discover the call by a growing experience of loss of purpose and meaning. What used to feel alive for us no longer does so; it becomes a pale shade of its former self. Old ways no longer provide fulfillment. We find ourselves yearning for a new way of living but may have no idea what that might look like. However, we become aware that something is changing, and once we find ourselves in transition, we have a choice of embracing the dynamics of growth or denying and resisting it and thereby stagnating. Life transitions involve three phases or sets of inner dynamics, which often overlap as we negotiate them.

Phase 1: Severance

If you recognize that you are entering a major life transition and you consciously choose to support that process, you need to do the work of severing yourself from who you have been in midlife adulthood. Severance is the first phase of the transition process and part of preparing for the journey into your life's next stage. It calls you to take stock of your life (who you have become, with your mix of strengths and weaknesses) as you seek to learn and distill wisdom from your many experiences. You will become aware of attitudes, fears, beliefs, behaviors, attachments, and self-identifications that may (or may not) have served you but will not do so in the future you hope for yourself. What deadens your aliveness and disconnects you from the wisdom and passion of your heart will need to be identified and shed, as a snake sheds its old constricting skin. You may experience grief that has been blocked. You may become aware of resentments toward others and yourself. All this is important so that you may move forward into elderhood without baggage that deadens your aliveness and blocks your energy and spiritual connection. With gratitude, you can celebrate your current life stage and begin to embrace your unknown future.

Phase 2: The Neutral Zone

This second phase of transition is identified by several names. Some call it liminal time (which comes from the Latin word for *limit*), which reflects the fact that during a successful transition process, you must encounter the limit of your former self and formally step beyond that limit. It is also called the threshold, indicating a crossing of a threshold from daily life into the world of the Great Mystery. Still others refer to this phase as the fertile void. Yet another term for this phase, and the one I use most often in this book, is *neutral zone*, first proposed by psychologist William Bridges in his excellent books on transition.

Throughout your transition process, especially during key times, you will find yourself thrust into the neutral zone, with its experience of being betwixt and between life stages. In this zone, there is no clear direction, although you may at time sense that the seeds of possibility for your elderhood have been planted in rich soil. In this phase you will find yourself alone, facing the uncharted wilderness within, with few familiar landmarks in sight and little that is safe and secure to hold on to. This is what Joseph Campbell called the hero's journey, undertaken since time immemorial by men and women with the courage to follow their inner calling. During this phase, you must face and conquer old fears before accessing the shining jewel of your true beauty and potential. Indeed, precious treasures are usually guarded by fearsome dragons. You may experience grief as you continue letting go of elements of your former identity while facing the fear that a new identity, a new sense of self and purpose, will never emerge. You will face the realization that ultimately you alone must find your calling and gifts; no one else can offer an authentic prescription for your life. As challenging as this phase may be, it is the necessary doorway to a new life chapter. In the neutral zone, the vision, creativity, strength, and spiritual connection that will define your elderhood will begin to emerge. They may be accompanied by gentle yet powerful stirrings of the heart. Their emergence may be punctuated by striking experiences of synchronicity, powerful dreams, or tear-laden heart openings. Perhaps it will be more subtle. However it happens, it can be life changing, pointing the way toward your future and empowering you as you grow into a new life stage.

You have many tools at your disposal during this neutral zone time. You may use fasting, prayer, solitude, meditation, drumming, journaling, close contact with nature, and any number of other practices and resources to facilitate a shift from everyday linear consciousness to the intuitive heart-centered modes of perceiving, through which your soul offers a vision of your unique callings and potentials. The neutral zone is a time for recognizing the limits of your personality and self; it's also for acknowledging that the conduit for the guidance and strength you need to move forward comes from your relationship with the Great Mystery (however you conceive of your divine source and essence). It is a time for "crying for vision" (the Native American concept the term *vision quest* is derived from). The most important quality you can bring to this phase is trust that the Great Mystery will support you in recognizing and realizing your potential for growth as a conscious elder.

Phase 3: Reincorporation

If you stay as conscious as possible throughout this process, you will begin to feel you have crossed some kind of a threshold. At that point you have begun to experience a change in your sense of identity. As the work of the neutral zone stage nears completion, reincorporation begins. This phase is also known as the return and the new beginning.

Ideally with the support of elders and the larger community, you will declare ownership of the fruits of your time in the neutral zone. Your reincorporation into the community is that challenging time when your task is to find ways to develop and use your emerging elder gifts to serve your sense of calling, for your own fulfillment, and as part of your contribution to the local and planetary community. In traditional indigenous societies, the community acknowledged the new status of those who made the passage into a new life stage, supported them in growing into this new role, and expected them to work to embody their gifts as fully as possible. In today's world, where there is no honored role for elders, you face the challenge of finding or creating a community with like-minded others. These people can affirm and support your commitment to an elderhood in which you do your best to bring your gifts to the larger community greatly in need of each and every conscious elder.

From Caterpillar to Butterfly

One of the most profound experiences in all my work with elder rites of passage was with a retreat group in Vermont. Over several days, we watched three caterpillars undergo transformation within a wire enclosure. The owner had carried them, along with bunches of the milkweed they fed on, from a verdant hillside to our group meeting room. For much of the time when we were not meeting as a group, we stood transfixed by these caterpillars. As each clung to a small branch, it gradually turned into a chrysalis, losing all its caterpillar characteristics. Each shed its skin and revealed a transparent ovular membrane filled with a green fluid. The caterpillar had entered its version of the neutral zone, no longer what it was but clearly not yet what it would become. That green fluid contained a pattern or image for the butterfly that would coalesce when the inner process was complete. We hoped that the butterflies would emerge before our retreat ended but knew that the process could not be rushed. As the days passed, we saw vague, indistinct forms develop within the membranes and watched as these ovals occasionally shook on their branches. On the final day of our retreat, as we were reflecting on what we had each learned about our own transitions, one chrysalis broke open, and a magnificent fragile, wet Monarch butterfly emerged. It needed an hour or so to dry its delicate wings in the sun. Shortly before our retreat ended, we opened the enclosure and it flew off to begin its new life. Soon thereafter we left to begin new chapters on our journeys toward conscious elderhood.

I close this chapter by returning to those committed people on that mesa in New Mexico whose rite of passage set the stage for this introduction to rites of passage and the process of life transition. They know, as does everyone who undertakes this inner journey, that the task of returning to everyday life after gaining a sense of what is possible is not easy. There are few societal structures in place to support their visions for growing older. The dominant culture's obsession with youth and newness will continue. Computers will generate more and more information, but wisdom will remain in short supply. The environment of our earth home will continue to be degraded. The media will continue to sell messages of fear. Yet the sun will continue to rise over those pinnacles to the east and shed its warmth on the mesa. The eagle will continue to soar overhead, seeing the big picture and calling all below to awaken. And ten more people will add their visions and voices to the emerging new understanding of the gifts that conscious elders can bring to a world desperately in need of elder wisdom and passion.

STORY BY THE FIRE
My Rite of Passage in Copper Canyon
by Joe H.

I grew up celebrating rituals. I was introduced to the Christian community through a ritual called baptism, and my first memory of ritual was the celebration of my First Holy Communion. As an adult, I was ordained to the Roman Catholic priesthood. In the context of a religious celebration, ritual at its core always has an aura of spirituality, and it certainly did for me. Its purpose is to be nourishing and nurturing as one moves through a journey of "passage."

Three years ago I found myself on another journey of passage in Mexico when I participated in a program called Meeting Ancient Wisdom. This program, offered by the Center for Conscious Eldering, gave me a unique opportunity to look inward at a time in my life when I realized I was growing old. The experience was a journey to the strikingly beautiful Copper Canyon complex in northern Mexico, the home of the Rarámuri people. As this indigenous people permitted us to look into their lives and deeply spiritual worldview, they helped us conscientiously search out within ourselves what is most essential so that we could get a clearer vision of all that we could be. What a profound experience our time with them was. It was there, with other pilgrims, including my wife, where I celebrated my passage from adulthood to elderhood. The journey brought me a new wisdom and unique awareness of my humanity as we interacted with our indigenous hosts and the breathtaking beauty of Copper Canyon. In the midst of it all, we used a ceremony of our own creation to mark and celebrate the elderhood we had all been gradually growing into for some time now.

We gathered as a knitted group of pilgrims in a beautiful historic villa that was very much in sync with its environment and situated on the floor of Batopilas Canyon, in the small town of Batopilas. Our minds and hearts burst forth with energy from meeting the ancient wisdom of a people completely aligned with the world that was theirs and for whom rites of passage were an integral part of living and dying.

As we prepared for our individual rites of passage ceremonies, we went inward to discern what the ceremony could best mean for each of us and what form the larger ceremony (and each of our personal ceremonies within it) should take. I determined that in my ceremony I wanted to make a connection with the rituals that were both personal to me and that I had celebrated for and with others. I asked Ron, Elizabeth (our other guide), and my wife, Margot, to support me by playing a role in my ceremony. Then the larger ceremony of passage began. The group offered our prayers, asking the Great Mystery to witness and support our work there.

When my turn came, as Elizabeth placed her hands on my head, Ron placed on my shoulders a handmade shawl my wife had procured from the Rarámuri and spoke to me of the elder wisdom that was mine to share when I returned home to Chicago. It was a holy moment, a memorable moment. I knew I was being invested by the divine with strength to be not just an elder but a wise, conscious elder. I now *knew* and trusted that I had grown into elderhood.

I anticipate that the years ahead are going to be like traveling through a maze. I will have to give special attention to each step I take. As a birthday card I once received expresses it, "You're not aging, you're evolving." I am now focusing on further evolving into the person who can use all my life experiences to continue to make a difference. My rite of passage in Copper Canyon empowered me to realize that I can indeed make a difference as I age.

3

NATURE AS HEALER
AND TEACHER

Conscious Eldering work is strongly grounded in recognition of the critical importance of nature—in the world outside human-created structures and environments and also within us—to our well-being and growth. As someone whose spirituality, growth, and service to others is deeply grounded in a living, conscious relationship with nature, I'd like to share my perspectives on the importance of such a relationship for those feeling called to conscious elderhood.

One of the key points throughout this book is that the role of elder is a *natural* archetypal role, deeply ingrained in the human psyche. The call to elderhood has found expression in virtually all human culture. This is true even today, in a modern world that has lost touch with nature, without and within. At the heart of conscious eldering lies a commitment to do all we can to prepare for answering this inner call. This is a much more difficult task than in yesterday's indigenous societies, where the process and the goal were clearly defined. It involves more than making slight modifications to our inner and outer lives as we age. It is deeply spiritual work, requiring vision that arises from our natural depths and empowerment that comes from tapping into life energies that are not easily found in human-created environments. A uniqueness of our retreats and workshops is that they are structured so that participants spend significant periods of time in nature, both as a group and in solitary reflection.

In their writing, James Hillman, Bill Plotkin, and others have stressed the distinction between spiritual paths and practices of ascent and of descent. The path and practices of ascent can lead to experiences of that formless universal Spirit, that Great Mystery known by many names, the Source and Essence of all creation. The goals of such practices are varied but tend to include a profound sense of oneness with the universal spirit; deep peace and joy; experiential realization that the essence of who we are is not our bodies, minds, and emotions; and the experience that the concerns of human life are transitory phenomena, while the world of the universal spirit is eternal. The path of ascent is critical to human growth and well-being, helping us recognize that we are spiritual beings having a human experience, rather than human beings striving to have spiritual experiences. However, ascent is only half of the spirituality needed to fulfill our potential for fully living in this material world as conscious human beings.

The other half is the spirituality of embodiment, the path and practices of descent, which focus on getting in touch with and working to embody the wisdom, gifts, and callings that come from the essential aspect of who we are. We call this aspect our soul, or the unique reflection of Spirit embodied in each person.

Our soul is that spark of the universal spirit in each of us that creates our individuality at the deepest level. It carries our unique calling and potential and the passion and energy to fulfill these. Our soul knows what is most important for us to learn in our lifetime and, for those whose worldview includes reincarnation, it is understood to carry the energetic imprints and karmas we bring into our lives. The experience of our essential soul makes possible the experience of interrelatedness with the essence or soul of all beings on this planet. This experience is the goal of the path and practices of descent, which are such crucial elements of indigenous wisdom, rites of passage, and conscious eldering.

In our modern Westernized world, for most people the quest for spirituality (which may or may not involve organized religion) is heavily focused on striving for ascent. It's about seeking experience of the world of spirit beyond material world concerns and/or living ethically to merit a joyous afterlife beyond this vale of tears. The path of descent does not deny the value of ascent (humans have striven for transpersonal experiences since the beginning of time), but, rather, it stresses the importance of recognizing and working to embody in *this* world, the divine potential inherent in all human beings. Embodiment comes not from looking without or following a set of ethical guidelines or commandments but from going within to experience the guidance and energy of our souls. This isn't about reflecting on concepts about our soul; it's about courting a living experience of the deepest, most essential dimension of ourselves. The older we get, the more difficult this process becomes for many. Our soul gets buried deeper and deeper beneath emotional scars, cultural messages, attachments to material things and views, and alienation from what is natural and authentic in ourselves and the world around us. As this happens, our vision dwindles, our passion fades, and our energy wanes. The work of conscious eldering is to gradually remove these layers and to create conditions that support our soul's expressions as we age.

Those of us who see the relevance of indigenous wisdom to the challenges facing individuals and societies in the modern world believe that inner work is critical to connect with our soul. The essence of indigenous wisdom is the understanding that all living beings and the earth itself are infused with a spiritual essence and life force. We humans best connect with that essence and life force in ourselves when we have a relationship with those same qualities in the natural world. And we best support the health of the natural world, which our well-being and very survival is totally dependent on by living in touch with that essential essence in us. We are not beings who are somehow above or different from nature just because we have minds and can conceptualize. We are as much nature as any animal or plant. The rhythms and cycles, deaths and rebirths, energies of chaos and organization that govern all the processes of nature are the same rhythms and cycles that rule the unfolding of our human lives. The more estranged we become from the experience of these cycles in the natural world, the more estranged we become from under-standing and experiencing these dynamics within us. The natural world, especially when we approach it consciously, reminds us (often in profound ways) of what is authentic and natural in us. It serves as a clear mirror, a healing contrast to all the clouded mirrors in city life that show us distorted, disempowering images of what the world tells us we should be.

Most people who attend our nature-based conscious eldering retreats say early on that a key factor in their decision to come was their memory of somehow being opened up by the natural world. They say that throughout their lives, their most memorable experiences of clarity, peace, guidance, and open-heartedness—their experiences of being in touch with who they sense they *really* are— have happened in nature. The clear mirror nature provides helps us get a glimpse of our own soul's radiance and helps us see with greater clarity those accumulated layers that must be removed before we can truly embody our sense of what is possible for us. Our urban lives tend to desensitize us and close down our sensitive hearts to protect us from being overwhelmed by the many non-life-supporting energies that assail us each day. The natural world tends to open our hearts to everything that is life enhancing. The more open our hearts are, the more easily trust and love can flow to support us in doing the healing work of conscious eldering.

A key mark of a conscious elder is a clear, strong sense of how we can best use our unique soul gifts and accumulated life skills and wisdom to be of service to a world in need. Skills inventories, re-careering classes, and other conceptual approaches can be useful in helping us get this sense of direction, but these alone may be insufficient for engendering clear vision and tapping the energies of passion that flow from our soul dimension. For many people, a key to passion-inspiring vision is an experience of having a deep, essential connection with other people, other living beings, and the earth itself. Through this experience of interrelatedness, we become aware on an intuitive heart-centered level (rather than just on a conceptual level) of how our personal qualities and gifts can best serve the greater good. Indigenous peoples have long known that the natural world catalyzes in people such experiences of interconnection. In contrast, modern Western society focuses on looking at individual components and pieces of information rather than interrelated systems and communities. Being in the natural world reminds us of wholes, of interdependency. It helps support the search for wisdom, which is often defined as understanding interrelationships and knowing how to use that understanding to support the greater good. It can help us know, intuitively, that our archetypal role of elder is crucial in supporting the greater whole of life and the life of our community. Claiming the role of elder isn't primarily about our own satisfaction, fulfillment, growth, or having something useful to do as we age, although it certainly encompasses these. From the eagle's-eye perspective, it is about serving life itself—spirit embodied in this world—as we develop experiential awareness of our importance in something much larger than our own lives.

In his groundbreaking book *Nature and the Human Soul*, Bill Plotkin presents a model for human development. In brief, Plotkin shows the process by which the human psyche, when properly supported, can grow through stages from early childhood through late elderhood. He paints a picture of how this would happen in a soul-centric society, which, emotionally and spiritually, would have much in common with many indigenous societies. He contrasts this with contemporary society, where this natural growth is often stunted or aborted. A critical insight is that true adults are people who have had soul-supportive childhoods and adolescences and have then been through the fires of initiation (rites of passage, both structured and spontaneous) to discover the life calling and spiritual empowerment that come from their soul. One can only get to this point by having a healthy, strong relationship with the natural world, without and within. Likewise, one can only become a true elder by first being a true adult. A great many people in midlife adult and senior bodies are emotional and spiritual children.[1]

The ideal is to be raised in a society that cultivates experiential recognition of nature and the human soul as embodiments of spirit. However, we need not despair if we have not been raised in such a society. Many of the deficits in our growth and the wounds in our psyches due to lack of nurturing can be healed by consciously choosing to do the kinds of inner work described in this book. We can make up lost ground by awareness and intention. We can, however imperfectly, let our elder within shine through. However, healing and nurturing our relationship with what is natural is an absolutely necessary part of this work.

Whether or not we have the benefit of being raised in a soul-centered society, when we approach nature consciously and reverently, seeking to experience and honor it as alive and infused with spirit, things often happen that confound our rational abilities and force us to seek explanations in the mysterious nonrational world of the soul. This is one of the primary reasons most rites of passage throughout history have involved intense immersion in the natural world. It was understood that rationality alone cannot provide the vision and spiritual empowerment needed to let go of a life stage, jump into the void, and incubate a new beginning—the process that is the very nature of human growth and development.

In everyday life, a butterfly flittering around us may not even be noticed, or if it is it may have no meaning for us. When we are sitting under a pine tree in a forest, working to move through the grief of losing a child and asking the Great Mystery for a sign that our child's spirit is somehow with us, and the only butterfly we have seen in days flutters close to our chest for several minutes, that is a life-transforming experience. When we are on a retreat in the desert and we are the only one who sees rattlesnakes—not once but twice—the experience can do more than any book or counseling session to help us understand our personal power. When we are on a mountain, filled with fear, and pray with all our hearts that the approaching thunderstorm not harm us, and the black clouds part, giving way to sunny weather, we *know* that we are supported by a power greater than our ego. We know we have received an incredible gift.

Our rational Western minds tell us that such experiences are just coincidences or that we are engaging in infantile magical thinking. But many other cultures know that this is not the case. They know that the material world and the world of our soul are connected in mysterious ways that psychologist Carl Jung and others called synchronicity. The outer world mirrors the inner world, with this correspondence being most easily seen when one is looking within while in nature and especially when engaged in a heartfelt ritual or ceremony. The hero's journey was, and is, a journey beyond everyday rational life into a mysterious realm where everything is perceived as sacred, interconnected, and meaningful. In this realm, there are no accidents or meaningless coincidences. Everything that happens—especially those happenings that stir something within us—has significance, and our role is to try to understand that significance. This understanding comes not from rational thinking but from the soul dimension, which speaks through synchronicity, dreams, feeling, imagery, and intuition. The seemingly magical happenings wake us up to a larger world, within and without. When we gain an experiential understanding of their significance, our lives are transformed.

If you gain nothing else from this book, I hope you gather some appreciation for how your growth can be greatly supported by choosing to mindfully spend time in the natural world (whether you aspire to conscious elderhood or just aging well). It need not be wilderness—just some place where nature's influence is stronger than human creation. Any growth work you do is supported by being in nature. Your well-being is supported by being in nature. In fact, an increasing number of psychologists inspired by Richard Louv's 2005 bestselling book *Last Child In the Woods* are now speaking of a disease called nature deficit disorder.[2] If you aspire to growing into the role of elder, your passage into this life stage may require significant time in a natural world that helps heal this deficit in you and show you what is natural, authentic, and life supporting in yourself.

STORY BY THE FIRE
Healing at a Pond
by Judith Helburn

Last night I returned to our cabin after a fire ceremony. We had begun our thirty-six hours of silence and were looking forward to a dawn-to-dusk solo in a self-chosen spot amid the magnificent spires and sandstone walls of Ghost Ranch.

Today I sit by the pond near the beginning of Box Canyon Trail. This small pond is alive with images—reflections from the golden cottonwoods edged by sage bushes releasing their tangy scent as I brush by. Their pale leaves and branches grow out of gnarly, twisted dark gray trunks and roots.

Clouds fill the sky, moving and changing both above and within the pond. The cottonwoods celebrate a presence greater than my small intrusion in their space. Birds chirp and bees buzz. It is cold enough that I move out of the shade into the occasional sun. Red earth marks my sun-spot seat.

I am in the fall of my life. It is autumn here at Ghost Ranch. Cottonwoods are releasing their golden gowns. Is it death? No, rather, change or transformation. Would I want to be the same—even tomorrow? Certainly not next year or even next month.

Watching the pond, I enter a reverie in which I see flows and shifts, movement both below the surface and within the reflections on the water. I see our retreat group sitting in council and speaking of our fears, especially of the fear of our changing bodies and minds. We praise the ancient beauty of this place and yet damn our aging bodies. Do we not see the absurdity of admiration for the ancients of our planet and fear of our own aging process? We, too, are part of the continuum.

As my physical facets and my mental facets slowly fade, they recede to make way for my shining spirit and heart. Stars that are invisible in the daylight of my life are made visible in the night. Does my mind accept that? No! "Me first and always," it chants. "I want to always be the most brilliant facet." Do I have a choice? Not really.

The pond has come alive as I sit at its edge watching dozens of tadpoles. Can there be a more blatant symbol of transformation? A water bug zooms into the school of tadpoles, leaving a wake and, perhaps, fewer tadpoles. The pond and the sky change as the sun rises to its zenith and hangs there for what seems like hours. The wind continues to keep me company, so much so that my "emergency rescue bell" hanging on a sage branch is singing. We need no rescue now.

I take a walk across the path and see huge boulders, many with memorial plaques placed there by the retreat center, and one small tombstone with a barely visible carved Star of David. It is a place of remembering. I didn't really think of that when I chose this spot. What in me has gone? Impatience and judgment, I hope. More likely, because of a sacred vow, now is the beginning of their demise.

As the sun arches across the sky, I move my seat, beginning near dawn in the East and ending near dusk in the North. The shadows grow longer, and I look over my shoulder as the sun slips behind the mesa. I retrieve my bell, empty my water bottle as an offering to the high desert, and head back to my cabin. The silence continues until the morning gathering and telling of our stories.

When it is my turn, I say, "A woman came to a desert paradise longing for solitude, for a time of being in beauty. She found, to her surprise, that she can have solitude while being alone but also while in community filled with respect, generosity, and ritual. Being in both types of grandeur with a sacred purpose magnifies her spirit to over-flowing. She brings back from her solitude a sense of being, a serenity and acceptance of her aging she can carry back to her city life. A deep, deep calmness has settled within, punctuated with flashes of quirky human behavior and laughter."

4

NO REGRETS: HEALING THE PAST TO EMPOWER THE FUTURE

I n 2005, after three years of cocreating and coguiding rite of passage retreats into conscious elderhood with Wes Burwell and Ann Roberts, I sensed there was much more to learn about this path and commitment. I had this momentous dream one night: I had been chosen to play the lead role in a mystery play. The atmosphere is deeply sacred and highly charged, since this is a ceremonial enactment of some of the deep wisdom at the heart of the world's great spiritual traditions. My role is to represent human beings at the doorstep of death. I am learning on behalf of all these mortals how to cross this threshold into the Great Unknown with an open heart, free of emotional encumbrances from the life that is about to end. I understand that I am not literally about to die at this time, but, rather, I am intended to symbolically learn what it means to prepare to die well.

In a great hall dimly lit by torchlight, monks garbed in orange and red carry me on a bier. They take me to several stations so I can learn something important about preparing for death. As I encounter the first stations, I am not very surprised by what I learn. (Upon awakening, I did not recall much about them. What I did recall was that my experience was one of being reminded of truths I already knew, such as the importance of making amends to those I have hurt and having the courage to do tasks that are important to me while I am still alive.)

Eventually, I am carried to the last station. The energy intensifies, the atmosphere feels electric. A booming voice resonates throughout my being: "No regrets. You can have no regrets. You must teach no regrets."

I woke, deeply shaken. I visited the bathroom, feeling like I was still in the dream. I returned to bed and immediately fell back into the dream—"No regrets. You must teach no regrets." I try to understand what it means—I must teach no regrets. Somehow this idea has something to do with choosing what promotes aliveness.

Then the dream shifts. I am with my beloved teachers of the art and practice of wilderness rites of passage, Steven Foster and Meredith Little. We are at an outdoor amphitheater where they are teaching a large number of people who listen to them with rapt attention. When their presentation is complete, they turn to me and say, "Ron, now it is time for you to teach 'no regrets.'" Knowing that I must somehow do this, I try to begin. Most of the crowd is leaving; the few that remain can't hear me due to the wind and other distractions; I am filled with frustration. I stop, and Steven tells me, "You can only teach 'no regrets' if you truly understand and are able to live without regrets."

This dream was alive in my awareness for the rest of the day and many days thereafter. This was probably the most powerful dream I have ever had and the most important message I have ever received from my inner guidance. This dream was, and continues to be, my mandate from the Great Mystery to engage in the work of teaching conscious eldering and to do the inner work that is absolutely necessary if my teaching is to be authentic and effective. It was this dream, when I was fifty-seven, that led me to know that engaging in conscious eldering work for my own growth and as the foundation for guiding others was to be my calling in the elder third of my life. This book is a reflection of the dream's mandate to work to understand, to embody in my life, and to teach the deepest meaning of "no regrets." The process is ongoing, as my understanding deepens and as I learn from others on the journey of conscious eldering.

One of the big catalysts for my deeper understanding of the meaning of "no regrets" occurred a year after this dream. I was attending a week-long workshop in Death Valley led by Meredith Little and Dr. Scott Eberle, who had served as the hospice physician for Steven Foster the year before as he prepared to die from an inherited lung disease. Scott is a talented rite of passage guide as well as a guide for people nearing the end of their lives. This workshop, called The Practice of Living and Dying, was for physicians, nurses, and hospice workers as well as guides of wilderness rites of passage—all of whom help people who are preparing for major passages.

The key understanding I gained from this highly experiential workshop was this: the inner work that prepares people to leave this life at peace, with open hearts and without the emotional baggage accumulated over a lifetime, is the same work that enables people to identify with midlife adulthood and move beyond it, without emotional baggage, so they can begin to embrace the role of elder with open hearts and clear energy. Each of these situations is (for the

psyche) a death to an old way of being and an entry into a new territory full of mystery and unknowns.

Several months after this important workshop, its key message was reinforced when I faced my mortality. I had been
praying for experiences to help me convert the powerful conceptual understanding from the Death Valley workshop into a visceral
experience that would deepen the foundation my growing commitment to guide others in conscious eldering was built upon.
The wise adage certainly applied to me: "Be careful what you ask
for; you may receive it in ways you don't expect." I was offered a
temporary position as program director at our local senior center.
I gladly accepted the opportunity, as I wanted to get to know
better a different cross section of seniors than those who came to
our conscious eldering retreats. Many of the seniors who came
to this center were in poor health and had various disabilities. Most
had few social connections. Lunch at the center seemed to be the
primary, (sometimes only) source of meaning for many of these
older people.

Only a couple of days into the job, I experienced the initial
arrhythmias that led to the diagnosis of a tumor in my lung and
subsequent biopsy and surgery. The many gifts I received from this
difficult experience included gaining appreciation for the reality
that in order to shine as an elder and to model what I teach, I need
to transform fears, heal relationships with others and with parts of
myself, and rewrite the disempowering stories I tell myself about my
life and my experiences. In short, at a gut level I grasped the need
to heal my past in order to move unencumbered into my future as a
conscious elder. I had to be as prepared as possible to leave this body
at that unknown time when death came calling. My understanding
of the power of working with regret was greatly enhanced by this

encounter with my mortality, which more than one teacher of mine has called "a transformative healing crisis."

Life Review Is the Key to Healing the Past

The mainstream view of aging seems to hold that people with gray hair who develop some measure of elder wisdom do so simply by living many years and having many experiences. It also says that life's inevitable wounds, if they can heal, do so naturally, without effort. "Don't dwell in the past," many say, "because there's nothing you can do to change it. We all have scars. Live as best you can now. Accept that idealism is for the young, who haven't yet borne the slings and arrows of outrageous fortune."

In sharp contrast, conscious eldering sees great value in examining the past. It holds that true wisdom is the result of experience consciously reflected upon and that the past can be healed so that we can age with clear, strong energy and an idealism informed by experience. Rather than being symbols of how life has beaten us down, the scars we carry can be testaments to how we are like the tree that, even with its scars, covers itself with new growth every year.

Life review is the foundation for much of the inner work of conscious eldering. It is our opportunity to come to terms with where we have traveled to reach this point of departure into a new chapter. It is the way that we recall our often long-forgotten experiences and bring to awareness what we learned—or still have the opportunity to learn—from those events. Life review helps us become aware of aspects of our past that may seem like vague images in our memory, consigned to the realm of the unconscious but that continue to exert a powerful influence on our lives. They may be experiences of loss that have never been fully grieved, of wounds that have not healed, of resentments that have not been forgiven—all of which sap our energy, close our hearts, and dull our light as we age. These may also be experiences of joy, compassion, idealism, strength, heroism, and divine support (perhaps forgotten) that can serve as sources of inspiration, reminding us what is best in ourselves and in life.

There are many ways to engage in life review. For example, you might break your life into seven segments and examine each one. Imagine your life encompassing the cycle of a year, with January being your first seven years; February, ages eight to fourteen; October, ages sixty-four to seventy; and December, seventy-eight plus. Other possibilities for life review include looking at your life with a focus on particular themes. You might consider writing an autobiography in which you tell the story of your life's most significant events and lessons to your children or descendants. You could ask a friend to do oral history work with you and use video to capture you telling your stories. Other ideas include participating in life review workshops and utilizing life review resources, which can be found on search engines. The possibilities are endless and just calling for your creativity. For example, in an excellent article written for the journal *Itineraries* titled "The Family Quilt: Harvesting and Sharing Life's Wisdom," Steve Harsh movingly tells of how his grandmother created a quilt composed of symbols of the landmark events in the life of his family and how she used this quilt to tell the story of her life.[1]

However you do life review work, what is most important is to recall key experiences and reflect on what they mean for you now. Review work is largely about the insights or new understandings that emerge as you reflect. Perhaps these experiences point to actions you need to take to help heal your past or to stories you have created about your past that need to be rewritten as you bring a broader perspective to your life. Your review may make you aware of strengths you need to cultivate, and it may get you in touch with still-alive embers of old dreams or passions that call to be rekindled.

Two powerful forces operate in each of our lives to shape who we become as we age. One of these is the past. With conscious effort, we have the ability to heal and learn from our past so that it becomes a source of strength and wisdom in our elder years. The other force is that deep calling—the sense of how we can come most alive through sharing our gifts—that is encoded in our souls and works to lead us toward its fulfillment. An important aspect of conscious eldering is our intention and work to gain ever-clearer access to this calling. The heart opening that results from healing our past is crucial in hearing our soul's calling and having the life energy to respond to it as conscious elders. Regret is grounded in the past. Revisiting and healing that past so that our journey toward fulfillment of our potential is unimpeded is central to approaching our life transitions with no regrets. The next four chapters will teach you how to consciously work to set yourself free.

STORY BY THE FIRE
Reflecting on My Past to Prepare for My Future
by Jonathan Parker

My intent is to use this week as a rite of passage to move my experience of life from one of struggle and much healing to one of peace and acceptance, joy and grace, and service to others. My intent is to move away from a state of living in fear to a state of conscious living in joy and wonder. I have come to this retreat to experience peace of mind, fill my senses with the wide, colorful scenic vistas of the Southwest, rest my mind in meditation, suspend all thought, cross thresholds into other states of consciousness, and connect spiritually, heart to heart, with like-minded seekers on this path of discovering our unfolding awareness of the aging process.

My physical body is tired. My mental processes have slowed to a crawl. My emotions have yanked me up and down like a yo-yo. My spirit cries out for respite. I need the clear, fresh high-altitude air to fill my lungs, caress my face, and purge my body of all the fears and negative emotions of the last several years. I have come here to watch the sun rise and set, and the stars slowly fill the night sky until they blanket the sky in a milky way. I have come here to wonder and wander. I have come to laugh. I have come knowing I will cry.

I have come to share my life experiences and to listen to others'. I have come to reflect upon my life, my actions, my motivations, my temptations, my struggles, my desires, my triumphs, and my failures. I have come to cure my disease of loneliness and discover the source of the profound feelings of aloneness I sometimes experience as well as the depression and anxiety that accompany these feelings. I am here, not running away from my past but seeking understanding and acceptance of my past. I am here in this special place to turn and face my life as it is up to now, to let go of regrets and attachments to my past, either negative or positive, and to leave the retreat at week's end with the ability to reorient my life's journey toward new directions and new destinations. I arrived feeling isolated, alone. I will leave feeling connected, part of a greater whole.

I am becoming conscious of entering the third great phase of my life—my elder years. My physical body is clearly announcing it on a daily basis. No longer does my mind respond to my commands for retrieval of facts and figures as it once did only several years ago. At age fifty-seven, I sense what I hear many of my older friends perceive as the cognitive losses they are becoming sensitive to as they age. Because of brain surgery to remove a malignant brain tumor and the subsequent maximum radiation treatment to my brain and the additional chemotherapy treatments I underwent fifteen years ago, I suspect that my current cognitive struggles and frustrations have come somewhat earlier to me than to most people I know.

Sensing a possibly shorter lifespan, I am motivated now at an earlier age than many to begin my process of conscious eldering, reorienting my life from being outwardly focused toward inner exploration, utilizing the techniques of life journaling, sharing life stories, reflection, meditation, and contemplation, among many other techniques. The questions foremost in my mind are, Have I lived my life as I should have? When I am close to death, will I have regrets, looking back on the life I lived? What can I do with the rest of my life?

Along this path of life review, I hope to identify what has brought me meaning and joy in my life up to now and what can bring me even more meaning and fulfillment in the remaining years of my life. While I need to continue my career as an electrical engineer, at least on a part-time basis, I know I must approach it in a radically different way, and I intend to do so. I doubt that any of my questions will be fully answered by the time I leave this retreat at week's end. Perhaps they never will be. I do believe, however, that after much contemplation and personal sharing, I will, by the time this retreat ends, arrive at a place of greater peace and acceptance of my life and whatever answers to my questions I do receive.

5

THE WORK OF FORGIVENESS
AND GRIEF

At the beginning of one of our Choosing Conscious Elderhood retreats, a woman in her early sixties shared her intention for the week by relating her experiences with two people she knew. The first was a woman in her late seventies who found no joy in her life. She was bitter and angry and let everyone know it. Her life seemed to be filled with complaints, negative judgments, accusations, and diatribes about how unfair life and other people had been to her. Being around her was a real downer; her negative energy rubbed off on everyone, so they did their best to avoid her.

The other woman, in her eighties, was someone everyone loved being around. Although she had lost her mobility and much of her sight, she was like a beacon of light. She never complained and found joy in little pleasures. People who spent time with her found that she was totally present with them. Her kind words and the love people felt from her always lifted their spirits. She had faced many difficulties in her life, but they were not the events she talked about. Rather, she tended to express gratitude for the kindness people had extended to her and the joys life had given her. She always had so much dignity. The woman at the retreat said that she hoped to learn how she could age like her kind, peaceful friend and not like her bitter acquaintance.

Aging seems to accentuate the best or the worst in us. The emotional and spiritual health (or lack thereof) we bring to our elder chapters is magnified by the dynamics of aging. Our unrecognized and unprocessed shadow elements—aspects of ourselves hidden from our conscious awareness—tend to become harder to suppress as our physical and emotional energy naturally decline. At the same time, our inner peace, joy, and light have the opportunity to flow more freely than ever if they are not smothered by unhealed emotional baggage. For most of us, work with forgiveness and grief is the most important and most difficult determinant of our emotional, spiritual, and often even physical quality of life as we age.

Rosemary Cox, a wise teacher of conscious aging who offers highly impactful workshops on forgiveness, says that forgiveness is the hardest chord to play in the human concerto. I imagine that most of us would agree. Resentment and forgiveness are the central dynamics in complex human dramas that include wounding others and being wounded ourselves, closing and opening hearts, balancing justice with compassion, and seeking to find meaning in life's painful experiences. How we deal with these dynamics throughout our lives, and especially as we approach elderhood, greatly influences who we become in our elder years. Yet most of us do not understand these complex dynamics. We know that hurting or being hurt by others strikes a painful blow that often leaves long-lasting wounds. We also know that awareness of the pain of these wounds often (but certainly not always) diminishes over time. We see forgiveness as a kind of moral imperative that may or may not be possible for us, especially when our anger and resentment feel justified and the offender does not demonstrate sincere contrition or has not been sufficiently punished.

What most of us do not understand are the true dynamics of forgiveness—that lack of forgiveness hurts us more than the one who has wounded us; that forgiveness does not somehow justify the act that caused the pain; and that forgiveness is a process that usually requires much more than an act of will.

Being hurt by another person causes us pain and generates anger and feelings of betrayal and resentment. For relatively small hurts, reconciliation may happen quickly if both parties make sincere efforts to repair the harm done. However, in many cases, especially when the wounds are significant, reconciliation does not happen, and the wounded party carries hurt feelings for years or decades. In such cases, with the passage of time these feelings may (or may not) lessen in intensity or drop below surface awareness, but they remain alive, fed by valuable life energy that could be used for empowering our highest ideals and positive emotions. All it takes is some unexpected catalyst—perhaps seeing the offender or being in a situation that reminds us of our wound—to cause these feelings to roar back to life, starkly reminding us that nothing has really changed or been healed. Forgiveness is so difficult because the feelings that result from being wounded can be so raw, so powerful, so tangible, so justified, and so righteous. Over time, we may come to consider these feelings as preferable to feeling vulnerable with no control and/or being numb.

What we don't recognize is the harm that holding on to these feelings does to us. There is a Buddhist adage that expresses this well: Holding on to resentment is like picking up a hot coal with our hand with the intention of finding an opportunity to throw it at the one who has hurt us. Another powerful image is that of believing that our ongoing resentment is somehow putting the offender in prison, when we are actually the ones imprisoned by our anger and closed hearts. The reality is that most of the time our lingering resentment has little if any effect on the offender but a big effect on us. I became acutely aware of this a few years ago when, in exploring the workings of my emotional life, I examined my relationship with a person I felt ongoing resentment toward. In doing so I saw how the feelings of anger, hurt, and resentment that arose whenever I was reminded of him felt toxic to me. As someone who has worked hard to open my heart, I saw how this lingering resentment, rather than helping me, only served to close my heart. That pain was greater than anything the actions of this other person had caused. I realized that healing was needed and consciously worked to support this process in myself.

Understanding Forgiveness

How can we work to create true forgiveness and healing? To undertake this process, we must first understand several things about forgiveness, which Rosemary Cox enumerates in her workshops:

- Forgiveness *does not* mean forgoing one's right to hurt feelings.
- Forgiveness does not change the past and does not mean that we forget the past; there may always be pain when we remember how we have been hurt or have hurt another.

- Forgiveness is not equated with losing, as if by forgiving one somehow loses and the offender wins.
- Forgiveness does not in any way excuse the act that did the wounding.
- Forgiveness does not absolve the offender from karmic or legal consequences of her wounding actions.
- Forgiveness does not mean that we will resume a relationship with the other person, although such reconciliation may be possible and right. It may well be the case that for our emotional or physical protection, a further relationship just can't happen.
- Forgiveness is a multilayered process rather than a single act, a process that may have to be repeated over and over, each time unraveling another layer and becoming more complete.

What forgiveness does is enable us to fully experience the pain of the hurt and then let it go, giving the karma of the wounding act back to the offender, where it belongs. While forgiveness does not mean forgetting the past, it does open up the future rather than keeping us emotionally stuck in a past that cannot be changed. Forgiveness opens the heart to unconditional love so that we can use the power of love to heal ourselves, and perhaps the offender, rather than stewing in a toxic mix of disempowering emotions and blocked heart energy. Forgiveness decreases physical and emotional stress. It allows us to take our power and control back from the other person so that our happiness is dependent on our choices, consciousness, and well-being, rather than on another who may or may not have any interest in true apology or reconciliation. And forgiveness enables us to begin to learn how our wounds, as terrible and unjustified as they may be in some cases, can help us create and support a life story of ongoing growth rather than victimhood.

On our retreats and workshops, we place a significant emphasis on forgiveness. With our participants, my colleagues and I explore the various dimensions of this process in group discussions and through practices that support forgiving. What we have learned is very much in accordance with the understandings of various theorists who write about the stages of the forgiveness process. The exact number of stages is not what's important. It is important to realize that while these stages tend to unfold somewhat sequentially, in reality this is more of a dynamic, complex process than a linear one, with elements of the various stages likely to appear at any time as we unravel and heal hurtful experiences of the past. In fact, rather than referring to them as stages, it might be more useful to see them as critical elements in the forgiveness process. The elements of forgiveness are generally recognized as uncovering and feeling what happened, committing to forgive, humanizing the offender, honestly examining your role in the offense, and forgiving (and continuing to forgive). Although these elements may overlap as they occur, it is important to remember that each one of them is crucial to the forgiveness process.

Elements of Forgiveness
Uncovering and Feeling What Happened

True forgiveness cannot happen unless you are able to fully know what it is you want to forgive. As time goes on, what you remember may only be the tip of a larger iceberg. You need to take time to bring awareness to the painful situation. This means looking at it as completely and objectively as possible, using all your senses to recapture the situation. Who did what in that situation? Try to relive what you were feeling in your emotions and in your body. Try to remember what you were thinking. What words were you hearing?

Feel the pain, the sense of loss or betrayal, the anger, the helplessness. Don't be afraid of fully entering the memory. Your intention to move toward forgiveness will protect you as you enter these painful depths.

Committing to Forgive

Ultimately, forgiveness is a choice you make, but it is a choice that in most cases requires you to do significant inner work if it is to bring healing to your deepest layers. The act of forgiveness may feel like jumping off a cliff, like you're giving up a familiar yet toxic and restrictive way of relating to another to enter unfamiliar emotional territory. Letting go of resentment can mean letting go of something that has begun to feel like a part of you. It is important at this point to remind yourself of the value of doing the work that leads to forgiveness—of the unburdening, the healing, the heart opening, the liberating, the self-empowering that can be the fruits of forgiving.

Humanizing the Offender

Try to separate the hurtful act from the person who did it. This does not justify or excuse the act. What it does is provide an opportunity to walk in the offender's shoes and allow some compassion and empathy to enter the process. What might the other person have been experiencing internally and externally? In what ways has he wounded, and how did he carry that wounding into his relationship with you? It may be the case that—for reasons you don't know—it is extremely difficult for him to offer genuine apology and make amends. Ask yourself if these same things go on in you when the table is turned.

Honestly Looking at Your Role
in Relation to the Hurtful Situation

In many (but certainly not all) situations that involve hurt, the dynamics are more complex than the wounded would like to admit. In such cases, it's often true that it takes two to tango. It is important that you look at your role in the situation as objectively as possible. Did you play a part in creating a dynamic that resulted in your being hurt? Perhaps shadow qualities in you fed shadow qualities in the other party, resulting in that person's hurtful actions. Did you bring unrealistic expectations to the relationship, thus setting you up for being or feeling hurt? What would the other person say about your role in the situation and are you willing to try to place yourself in her shoes?

Whether or not you can see yourself having any responsibility for the wounding action, you do have responsibility for how you relate to it. Becoming more conscious of this enables you to see this level of responsibility. When you are conscious, you will see that you can allow your wounds to create or support a personal story of yourself as victim, forever at the mercy of painful events. Or you can allow the wounds to help you understand a story of continual growth— a story where you use all your experiences to gain strength, increase self-awareness, become more resilient, and get in touch with the personal gifts and qualities that these painful stories potentially enable you to recognize and tap. In your own way, you can be a wounded healer rather than a victim. The more conscious you become, the more you recognize that this is your choice and that forgiveness is critical in making this choice. When you reframe the hurts you have experienced in this way, true forgiveness becomes easier and more likely.

Forgiving and Continuing to Forgive

Forgiving is an act of courage and will. It is an act performed internally but one that can be reinforced by external action. If the one who has hurt you is willing and available, an outward expression of forgiveness from him can make the process even more healing for you. It may also bring important healing to the other person, who may be carrying remorse and guilt for what happened and may even be feeling that forgiveness is impossible. Such a meeting can give you the opportunity to express your pain and can provide the other person with the opportunity to express sorrow at having hurt you, ask for your forgiveness, and find some way to make amends if possible.

If this person is not available to receive your forgiveness in person, the opening of your heart still sends the healing energy of love to that person's spirit, a gift that may be significant in ways you may never see. As you open your heart, it can be helpful to periodically imagine a golden light enveloping you and the one you are forgiving, sending your blessing as the other person grows toward wholeness. Remember, forgiveness is a process with many layers. You may forgive as completely as you think you can today, only to find that deeper layers reveal themselves tomorrow. As with all the inner work of conscious eldering, forgiveness is an unfolding process that requires commitment to the ongoing deepening of your consciousness.

When You Are the One Who Needs to Be Forgiven

These five elements are equally important when you are the one who has inflicted hurt. Rather than carrying remorse or guilt without true awareness of the situation, it is important for you to uncover and deeply feel what happened, acknowledge and try to understand your role in it, have the courage to ask the one you have hurt to forgive you, and do whatever you can to make appropriate amends. Whether the other person is able or willing to forgive you or not, it may well be the case that forgiving yourself is critical to your healing and may be even more critical than receiving the other's forgiveness.

For many of us, self-forgiveness is the most difficult form of forgiveness. We are our own harshest critics and judges, often finding it much easier to extend compassion and understanding to others than to ourselves. Yet closing our hearts to ourselves compounds any harm we have done to others by inflicting harm on ourselves. In a great many cases, what needs self-forgiveness is not harm done to others but personal weaknesses or perceived choices or actions that we feel have damaged our own lives. It is so easy to use these weaknesses or poor choices to justify feeding disempowering personal stories that label us as unworthy, inadequate, or flawed. Self-forgiveness depends upon our willingness to carefully examine our choices and actions and, in many cases, acknowledge that we did the best we could with the awareness we had at the time. If we see that we did not do the best we could, it requires that we use our regrets not to berate ourselves but as important guideposts on our journeys into a positive, conscious future. The biggest catalysts for our growth are often (perhaps mostly) what we learn from our mistakes, weaknesses, and poor choices. The biggest impediments to growing can be the self-denigration that positions these weaknesses as evidence of unworthiness and reasons to close our hearts to ourselves.

It is also worth noting that in the bigger picture—the soul's eye view of our lives—things are often not what they seem. What may seem to be mistakes or poor choices from the perspective of our ego and culture may be (from our soul's perspective) what needs to happen to move us forward on our unique life paths. Rather than forgiveness, what may be needed in such situations is honoring ourselves for making difficult yet important choices.

Just as unforgiven hurts close our hearts and bind the life energy that could empower a positive future to painful experiences of the past, unfelt, unprocessed grief is equally debilitating but with slightly different mechanics. Grief—the pain of losing someone or something we dearly love—is a powerful emotion that needs to be honored, felt, expressed, and understood after we suffer loss. When this understanding happens, we naturally move from the pain of loss to healing and acceptance as an integral aspect of the experience of being human. When this does not happen, we either remain stuck in grief, unable to move forward, or become emotionally numb as the pain of loss is stuffed deep inside, unable to find the healthy expression it needs.

We live in a modern world that is uncomfortable with the authentic, healthy expression of "negative" emotions in general. Grief is treated as a necessary evil, something to be allowed for a short time after significant loss but then gotten past as we return to being productive as soon as possible. However, suppression of the grief of loss only serves to imperil our emotional well-being as individuals and the well-being of our society. We can't be vital, energized elders when our life energy has been numbed by being shoved deep inside. Most of us would prefer to be able to strongly experience the positive emotions of life—joy, optimism, inspiration, excitement—without having to feel the difficult, painful emotions. But that just isn't possible. The reality is that if we are to fully experience our positive emotions, we have to be emotionally alive, and that means experiencing the complete range of our emotional repertoire. We are either emotionally alive or, to a greater or lesser degree, emotionally numb. As they age, a great many people lose their zest for life and their optimism and excitement about their future due to an ever-growing emotional numbness.

The grief that follows loss can be one of life's most transformative experiences, and this is especially the case if we bring consciousness to our grieving. Grief cracks us open, breaking down the external and internal structures that enable us to function effectively in "normal" times. With our ego cracked open by loss, the pain and disorientation that ensues shows us the limitations of the ego we identified with to that point. They force us to go deeper to find the inner resources needed to live with and move forward from our grief. Those who have become conscious of the transformative potential of transition are able to understand their grief as a doorway to growth into a new chapter in their lives.

Significant, painful loss is indeed for many the catalyst that begins a personal life passage, albeit one we have not invited and may feel unprepared for. Our loss severs us from a previous chapter and thrusts us into uncharted waters with few if any dependable maps: no shore in sight, no idea when this exile from our "normal" life will end, and no one there to rescue us. We find ourselves in the neutral zone of a personal life passage. While conceptual understandings seem incapable of providing relief from the grief and disorientation that fill this space, the more conscious we become of the universal dynamics of human transition, the better able we are to trust the process that is working through our unique personal journey from loss through grief to a new beginning. There is no prescription for navigating through the rough seas of grief. The journey is as unique as each of us. However, based upon my personal experiences, the experiences of our retreat participants and coaching clients, and wisdom from friends and colleagues who work with hospice, I have collected some general guidelines, the first of which is understanding the five stages of grief.

The idea that there are five stages of grief is strongly embedded in our current culture. The reality seems to be that while these five "stages" describe dynamics that arise for most people after significant loss, they often don't happen sequentially. Loss produces suffering, the overriding experience of the grief process. Denial, anger, bargaining, depression, and acceptance—the five "stages" of grief described by Elisabeth Kübler-Ross—are elements that arise within the context of our suffering but not necessarily in a particular order, not always just once, and often not of equal strength.[1] They are part of a complex web of inner dynamics unique to each individual. As we become more aware of our inner life, we are increasingly able to recognize these dynamics for what they are—a healthy part of our journey through grief and not something to fear or resist.

We facilitate our journey through grief by trusting that what is happening within us is part of our process of healing and growth and by allowing it to happen without fear that we will remain forever stuck in these experiences. Denying or suppressing these feelings may only serve to make us stuck. We keep the healing force most alive by allowing ourselves to feel and express our pain and suffering, however and whenever it shows up. Being supported and witnessed by unconditionally loving friends plays a critical role on this journey. Being able to share our experience with someone who shines the light of their love on our inner darkness and turmoil is the most significant aspect of our healing. I believe that many people who never truly heal from grief have not had the gift of having their grief witnessed by others who can lend unconditionally loving support.

How do you know when you have moved through your grief process after a significant loss—whether of a loved one, a dream, a job, a career, a state of good health, or a life stage—and are substantially healed and starting to emerge into a new beginning? At some point, you start to become aware that your pain, disorientation, and hopelessness give way to a sense of emerging purpose and optimism. You can again feel alive and experience joy, although your life has significantly changed. You may begin to recognize that the important role formerly played by the lost person, thing, or identity can now be filled in some other way—not that you can "replace" who or what you have lost, but what they contributed to your well-being can be found in other sources. For example, perhaps the strength or loving acceptance you needed can begin to come from within yourself or from others who enter your life. Or perhaps the sense of identity and purpose you lost when you retired can be replaced by the passion that emerges as you claim the role of conscious elder-in-training.

Conversely, those who have not processed their grief often remain stuck in it for years and perhaps for the rest of their lives. They may remain mired in suffering and hopelessness with no light ever shining through. Or, as so often happens, their unacknowledged and unexpressed emotions will shut down their emotional and spiritual life, resulting in low-grade numbness or possibly serious depression. If you aspire to be a vital, optimistic, and spiritually alive elder, you cannot be emotionally numb.

Having moved through the passage of grief into a new beginning does not mean that the pain of loss is gone. That pain has become part of who you are—part of the rich texture of your human experience—and will likely arise many times in the future, when your memory of who or what you have lost comes into your awareness. But once you have made your new beginning, the pain is recognized as part of your emotional aliveness rather than as something that disempowers you or fills you with hopelessness. The pain of your grief can serve as an important reminder of your humanity, of your essential connection with all of the human family. It makes it possible for you to empathize with and be accessible to others as they suffer.

Grief serves another important role as it confronts us with the reality of death as an inevitable, natural, and transformative part of life. Whether it is the death of all humans, every other being that has life, the identities we carry throughout our lives, or our abilities, death is what makes new life possible. Becoming increasingly aware of our fears concerning death in all its manifestations does not mean overcoming them; it means finding more ease with being fearful of loss and the grief that follows. This awareness is invaluable in helping us consciously prepare for the losses that inevitably accompany aging, embrace these losses as opportunities for growth, and experience a peaceful passage from this life into whatever is next.

With a commitment to becoming increasingly conscious, most people can do the important work of forgiveness and healing grief on their own, using the loving witness of friends and family for support. I have seen people achieve tremendous breakthroughs with forgiveness and previously unhealed grief during weeklong retreats. As with all conscious eldering work, tapping the spiritual dimension plays a critical role in healing the past. This is the source of unconditional love that helps move the quest for healing from a primarily psychological process to one involving our whole being—body, mind, emotions, and spirit. However, many people, especially those who have experienced grievous loss, need the help of professional therapists or counselors on this healing journey. Part of being a conscious elder is recognizing when we need help and being willing to seek out and utilize that help. Having the courage and insight to seek the help we need to heal our past is a reflection of our strength rather than an indicator of weakness.

STORY BY THE FIRE
Facing My Fear of Death Through Forgiveness Work
by Helene Aarons

Several years ago, at the age of seventy, I left my full-time career. I had no plan for what I would do next but simply heeded an inner prompting to open to new changes in my life.

Having worked a highly visible product-oriented job for so many years, the sudden expanse of so much free and unstructured time was overwhelming. I was advised to make the emptiness my ally and listen to what it had to teach me. But it was too much, too quick. I even asked myself, "Did I retire too soon? Did I misread the guidance to let go, move on?"

I quickly realized that I needed professional help to deal with my fear of the emptiness, the void. In the course of doing this deep personal work, I ran smack into my fear of death and dying. And after a few months, I encountered a crossroads, a choice point. Would I choose to face and work to transform this fear of death and dying? Or would I continue living with my denial, numbness, and loss of contact with my inner guidance? I have probably lived 99 percent of my life from my head, willing myself from one experience to the next, putting my unpleasant feelings into boxes and filing them away. I was now seeing and experiencing how my fear of aging and death was keeping me a self-made prisoner, so afraid to surrender to my feelings, to let go of my need for control, to fully live. Instead I was choosing to live a "half-life" for the remaining years of my life.

Faced with this decision, I chose to fully live the rest of my life to the best of my ability. I started reading books—Rabbi Zalman Schachter-Shalomi's *From Age-ing to Sage-ing*, Stephen Levine's *A Year to Live: How to Live This Year As If It Were Your Last*, and Scott

Eberle's *The Final Crossing: Learning to Die in Order to Live*. I found people in my community who came forward to talk about death and dying. I signed up for several workshops, and in a retreat called Choosing Conscious Elderhood, I firmed up my commitment and ceremonially acknowledged that my spiritual path is to live my life as a conscious elder.

I could have chosen a number of entry points, but I am beginning to do my eldering work with healing my relationships and with learning and practicing forgiveness of myself and others. As I was making a list of key relationships in my life that require healing, I realized that there are three subsets of relationships I am dealing with: relationships with myself, with others still living, and with those who have died.

I started with myself. This made me feel less vulnerable, and I felt it would be good practice for doing this work with loved ones. I developed a list of actions and incidents in my life that made me squirm with shame when I recalled them. And then there were past situations that I had simply walked away from (an abortion and a miscarriage) without any conscious awareness. I could heal some of these "hurts" myself, but others would require professional help.

As I began to work on healing my relationship with myself (and I'm still working down my list!), I decided to also begin healing my relationship with others. One such incident involved a conversation with my former husband about something that had occurred more than forty years ago. When we began sharing our memories of the incident, it became clear that what I had remembered (and coated with shame) was not what had actually happened. I really hadn't been the awful person I remembered being. I felt the bubble of energy that had been trapped by my false story suddenly pop. Not only was our relationship healed around that incident, but it actually brought us into a present relationship based more upon honesty and a commitment to work together to clear up all the unfinished business between us. It feels so good to have a partner in this effort.

So I continue in my work, but now using the support of others I am also committed to aging consciously. I bring to it a renewed commitment and energy, to fully live each day of my life as best as I can and prepare for a good death when that time comes. Doing this work is helping me ease into my fears of death and dying and respect the fears that are becoming the most powerful teachers and allies I will encounter.

6

THE POWER OF STORY
TO SHAPE OUR FUTURE

A key aspect of our uniqueness as human beings is the need to find meaning in what we experience. We look for connections between the events of our lives and use our interpretations of these connections, whether accurate or not, to shape the stories that give us our sense of identity—of who we are, what we are capable of, and what our lives mean. There is immense power in story. We are story-creating beings who can't help but weave narratives about our lives and then tell these stories to ourselves and others. This process of story creation is largely unconscious and yet has the power to play the lead role in determining who we believe we can become and, therefore, who we indeed do become.

Stories are like magnets. Once the core of a personal story develops, most often as the result of childhood experiences, then a dynamic is set up, which we use to interpret subsequent experiences that have anything in common with the core tenets of that story as examples of its truth. We see the story as providing the threads that tie these experiences together, and we use those experiences to reinforce the story, giving it more and more strength in our psyche—and on and on. Since these stories over time become key to our sense of self, they don't just determine how we interpret our experiences; they also very much shape our experiences. What we believe about ourselves very much determines how we respond to situations, interact with others, make choices, create values, and understand life. And since they act like magnets, our stories tend to attract to us the people and experiences that serve to reinforce them.

The stories we construct to try to make sense of our lives are not merely mental constructs, because we are not merely rational beings. Most of the power of these stories operates below the level of conscious awareness, with strong stories becoming deeply ingrained in our emotions and bodies as well as our minds. As we move through life, we may develop some awareness of how our unproductive behaviors, negative thoughts, or poor self-image seem to undermine our best intentions, but all too often we don't understand the source and power of those dynamics that defy our attempts to change our feelings, behaviors, and self-image through willpower alone.

Our disempowering stories will continue to exert their strong influence until something happens with the power to cause us to question their validity and shift their energy in our psyches, emotions, and bodies. This something can be grace touching our lives via highly impactful experiences that shake up our self-image and turn our worldview upside down, giving us glimpses of a new, empowering story. This something can also be a conscious choice to work to become aware of the stories, both empowering and

disempowering, that we have created and live by. With this awareness, the next step is to honor and reinforce those stories that enliven
us and bring out our best and work to rewrite our disempowering
stories—to reframe the way we understand our painful life experiences. By doing so, the life energy that has been bound to stories of
victimhood, inadequacy, unworthiness, regret, and the like, keeping
them alive and powerful in us, is freed to support our growth and
the fulfillment of our potential. The conscious choice to rewrite or
recontextualize the stories that shape us is one of the most important
components of conscious eldering.

Life review is the process that enables us to become aware of
the stories we have created to define ourselves and understand our
experiences. As we look back on our lives with focus and careful
attention, we see patterns. Events and experiences that, over time,
have constellated into the stories that shape our behavior, attitudes,
and aspirations come into our awareness. Creating the opportunity
to look at our experiences with new eyes, we have more ability than
we had as children or younger adults to ascertain whether our origi-
nal interpretation of these experiences are indeed accurate and will
serve our well-being as we age.

This inner work of recontextualizing is much deeper than trying
to make lemonade out of the lemons life has tossed our way (although
lemonade certainly tastes better than sour lemons). Rather, this
work is about seeking a core-level understanding of the meaning of
our experiences and of how we can use all of them, both pleasant and
painful, to facilitate our growth into conscious elderhood. It is about
becoming conscious of inner dynamics and working to transform
them so that they don't sap our energy, dim our vision, and sabotage
our attempts to embody our noblest values and ideals. Conscious
eldering is about much more than just setting goals and intentions as

we age; it is also about becoming conscious of decisions and transforming the aspects of ourselves that stand in our way and are more powerful than our willpower in shaping our future.

Recontextualizing experiences can be done at various levels of depth. For experiences that had a relatively minor impact on you, approaching the process conceptually and looking for the silver lining in what caused you pain may be enough to cause a positive shift. However, the experiences with strong emotional impact that continue to drive a disempowering story require work on a deeper, more sustained level. Many of us are able to gradually, sometimes dramatically, transform our disempowering stories by doing the inner work recommended in this book. These stories are often rooted in painful experiences that require forgiveness and healing of grief before true recontextualizing can happen. For those of us who have experienced especially traumatic wounding, it may well be the case that we need the assistance of a professional counselor or therapist to help us heal. You may even seek the help of a body worker or energy worker to help heal the energetic wounding in your body. In any case, working to deepen conscious awareness of the spiritual dimension in ourselves is the key component in transforming our disempowering stories.

Conscious eldering work is, at its core, profoundly spiritual. It is work that seeks to connect us with the deep knowing of ourselves as spiritual beings living in bodies and having personalities that enable us to function in the world, but it is also about being much more than just these bodies and personalities. It is work that helps us know and tap into the power of the true story working to unfold throughout our lives. It is work that requires a deep trust, grounded in the spiritual dimension of ourselves, that the divine intelligence present in us has a purpose for our lives and is working through our experiences to achieve that purpose.

From the perspective of our egos, difficult, painful experiences are best avoided and generally don't have a positive function. They are negatives, and we build negative stories around them and their role in our lives. However, conscious eldering involves cultivating awareness of an eagle's-eye view that is much vaster and more acute than what our ego's eyes can see. All the spiritual traditions teach that when we open to our soul's awareness, we know that each of our lives has a purpose, a destiny that seeks to unfold through our unique set of life experiences, both pleasant and painful. We know that we can choose to use all our experiences to learn about our capabilities and gifts and grow into the people we have the potential to become. From this heightened awareness, we attribute very different meanings to our experiences than we would otherwise. We see that the disempowering stories we have created are not true and are just that—disempowering. This heightened consciousness has the power to heal wounds that painful experiences have inflicted on our bodies, minds, emotions, and spirits. It has the power to dissolve our disempowering stories and plant powerful seeds of new stories that free up our energy, awaken our vision, stir up our passion, and make us come truly alive.

The essence of recontextualizing is viewing our painful or difficult life experiences through the lenses of the highest level of consciousness we can access. Our intention is to gain understanding of how our experiences have contributed—or have the potential to contribute as we revisit them with conscious awareness—to our growth and learning. In the bigger picture of our life, the wound inflicted on us may have taught us compassion or empathy for the suffering of others. It may have taught us about our resilience or helped us learn something important about boundaries. As is often the case, it may have been the doorway through which our most important gifts emerge. The most powerful healers have been wounded themselves.

From the perspective of our souls, the hurt we inflicted on another may have taught us about our shadow side—a critical awareness if we are to grow as human beings. A career decision we made that we regret may have been a crucial step toward becoming who we are today, even if the mechanics are not obvious. The job we lost may have pushed us into a difficult search that led to a fuller expression of our gifts. Our difficult times may have helped us hone our cunning, flexibility, and resiliency. And they may have forced us to see the limits of our egos and turn inward to our spiritual depths for answers and guidance.

Recontextualizing helps us see these silver linings and is critical to having "no regrets" as we die to who we have been and move forward into the next stage of our journey. I want it to be clear that I am not suggesting that recontextualizing our experiences and rewriting our stories means we will eliminate painful memories. The slings and arrows did cause us pain. That pain is part of the story of our humanity. The pain will emerge at times, and we will likely remember and feel it when we do life review work. For most of us, regret is also part of our humanity. It is generally those actions or inactions of our own that caused pain to others or to ourselves that we experience as regrets. How we interpret those painful experiences and create stories around them has much to do with our relationship with regret. Our regrets can become potent elements of our disempowering stories, serving only to diminish our sense of self-worth as they continually remind us of our failures and flaws. Or they can become our teachers, reminding us of behaviors and attitudes that did not work for us in the past and won't work in the future and pointing the way to life-enhancing alternate behaviors and attitudes. Key to conscious eldering is striving to live and die with no disempowering regrets—honoring and loving ourselves as imperfect yet continually growing, learning beings.

But what if nothing that seems to need recontextualizing comes into awareness? What if you conclude that you don't have any disempowering stories that call to be rewritten? It's possible that you do not. However, once you commit to engaging in life review work, you may find that these sometimes painful memories arise even when you are not actively reviewing. Furthermore, as you increase awareness of your inner life, you will probably find yourself having moments when something triggers feelings in you that reflect the disempowering stories that lurk just beneath your consciousness. These may be feelings of being inadequate, a victim, flawed, or unworthy of love. Often, such memories evoke the strong feelings we had as children—the feelings that lie at the heart of disempowering stories. These feelings, especially if they are strong and leave us feeling uncentered and disempowered, are the clue that recontextualizing work might benefit us. For they are not just remembrances of childhood experiences but images and interpretations that continue, in subtle or not so subtle ways, to impact our lives. It takes courage to allow ourselves to feel these emotions, remember events that have evoked them, and work to see how we can relate to them as agents for our growth rather than as reinforcements for stories that do not serve us as we seek to bring our compassion and clear energy to our eldering.

The Hero's Journey

The work to move from midlife adulthood toward conscious elderhood has the potential to be a true rite of passage, requiring us to heal the past and let go of old self-identifications as we move forward with courage and trust into the unknown territory of our future. From the big-picture perspective of our souls, each of our lives is a hero's journey. We have the opportunity to continually learn from our past, build on the qualities that support our growth and fulfillment, and let go of beliefs and stories that only serve to weaken us. Then we can enter, without old disabling baggage, the realm of mystery and spirit where vision and empowerment for the future are found.

The work of recontextualizing our lives is greatly enhanced by remembering that as we enter life we are all called to enact our unique version of the hero's journey. In doing so, we are living mythically. Jean Houston, along with Joseph Campbell and others, has done much to help the modern world understand the power of myth. She wrote that myth "is story invested with all of our potentials and highest ideals, as well as our shadows and terrors. . . . It provides a template that allows us to open ourselves to the hidden capacities we had forgotten we had; the creative potentials we didn't know how to use; and the deeper knowing that transcends past, present and future—a deeper knowing that is within every one of us."[1]

However, living in a modern world that has little understanding of the mythical dimension of life, we tend to see our lives as individual small stories with no inherent meaning, largely shaped by random events and experiences. If the world's myths do indeed point to inherent meaning in our human experience, and if the hero's journey is indeed the master myth—the soul's template for the human process of growth—then our passage through life can best be understood as a highly meaningful journey involving sorrow and joy, loneliness and community, endings and beginnings, experience and learning—all toward the fulfillment of our unique human potential. Conscious eldering is about choosing to intentionally embark on the final chapters of our hero's journey, entering uncharted territory to discover our potential to bring the gifts of true elders to a world urgently in need. Recontextualizing helps us recognize and acknowledge ourselves as the hero or heroine going on the journey into elderhood. We are on the lifelong larger journey of unfolding our own personal myth.

STORY BY THE FIRE
From Regretting to Honoring
by Ron Pevny

I went to college in the 1960s. At that time, with the dramatic birth of the human potential movement, the anti-war movement, the awakening of environmental awareness, and other efforts to help all humans be accorded respect and the opportunity to thrive, an idealism that I did not know was in me came alive. But then I graduated, received a four-year fellowship in a clinical psychology program, and immediately assumed the next role my family and society expected me to fill.

Within a short time, I found that the program had no life for me. It focused heavily on that school of psychology called behaviorism, but I found myself becoming strongly attracted to humanistic and transpersonal approaches. As the end of the first semester approached, I felt trapped in a program that seemed to deaden my spirit, but when I began to contemplate leaving, I was filled with conflict. If I left, I would disappoint my parents, those who offered me the fellowship, and my image of myself as competent, disciplined, and grounded. I finally did decide to leave the program at semester's end. A few days later while driving across a beautiful mountain pass from where I lived to the university, as I was again rehashing my decision and remaining conflicted about it, the Beatles' "Let It Be" came on the radio. As it did so, I was blessed with the first peak experience of my life. The heavy clouds on the pass and within me parted, brilliant sunshine broke through, and for several minutes I experienced the deepest joy and peace I had ever known. I *knew* that I had made the right decision. I knew that my strong sense of calling to understand the interface between psychology and spirituality was real and that I must trust and follow that calling.

Back home in Colorado, however, all the conditioning that had originally led me to the graduate program asserted itself in a big way. Quite unconsciously, I applied for an innovative new PhD program in Social Demography at another university and received another full-ride fellowship. It did not take me long to realize that this program felt more deadening to me than the clinical psych program I had left, as it focused on research and numbers, while my strength and joy came from working with people. At the end of the first semester, I left that program and found myself wallowing in a three-year period of confusion, self-doubt, and self-recrimination. I took the only jobs I could find—low-paying ones that offered little or no fulfillment. At the same time, I experienced physical challenges that mainstream medicine could not address. These painful psychosomatic symptoms led me to meditation, study with healers, and experiential exploration of various approaches that had begun to intrigue me in my first graduate program. These were the three most difficult years I have ever experienced, with my occasional precious moments of trust and clarity overshadowed by a powerful and growing story of how I was irresponsible, undisciplined, and ungrounded, and had done irreparable harm to my life.

Then, in what felt like a moment of true grace, I discovered a master's program at the California Institute of Integral Studies that wove together the approaches to psychological and spiritual growth of the Eastern traditions and Western transpersonal psychology. My three years in this program and the following two years in San Francisco were a time of blossoming for me, as I was surrounded by teachers, approaches, and opportunities that healed my psychosomatic ills and brought me alive. It was during this time that I discovered the vision quest and my strong calling to serve others through work with wilderness rites of passage.

However, when I returned to Colorado, the disempowering story that had been lying dormant during those halcyon California years sprang back to life and exerted its pull for many years. I had few opportunities to do the work I felt called to. I spent many years doing jobs that paid reasonably well but brought me little fulfillment. In many down moments, I recalled the words of my parents who, as I struggled with those early graduate programs, told me that I was acting like an ungrounded dreamer and that if I didn't let go of my fantasies and follow the mainstream prescription for success, I would ruin my life. They told me that "the ship of opportunity comes once, and if you miss it you may never have another chance." Every unfulfilling job, every struggle, and every dark moment fed and reinforced the story of my irresponsibility and failure to make the most of my life.

I was blessed to have enough moments of clarity and spiritual connection to help me persevere through the hopelessness of those many difficult years. But throughout, my big, disempowering story sapped my energy and warred with my deepest knowing of my calling and potential, and I feared that I would forever have to live with the battle between this story and the clarity I experienced in my moments of heightened spiritual awareness.

As I began my personal conscious eldering work and guiding others in this work, life review became important to me. I tried to look with fresh eyes at my graduate school experiences, the decisions I had made, what was going on in me as I made the choices, my struggles after those decisions, and the moments of grace when light pierced through my darkness. I looked for patterns.

I learned several important things that have enabled me to dismantle my disempowering story. Perhaps most important, I saw how in my darkest times, I was blessed with enough experiences similar in quality to that "Let It Be" experience on the highway to keep the light of hope alive in me. At these times, I knew at the deepest levels of myself that my life has a purpose, that I am guided in fulfilling that purpose, and that my life journey of growth requires me to trust my sense of inner knowing rather than society's prescriptions. At those times of eagle's-eye consciousness, I knew that my life is and must be the hero's journey I teach.

As I reviewed my life, keeping my precious awareness of the big picture close at hand, I saw that if I had forced myself to stay in the programs I'd left, although they may have led to greater security and status, I would have violated my young, still-tender recognition of what had brought me alive, and perhaps would have deeply wounded myself. I saw that my commitment to honoring my sense of calling demonstrated great responsibility, groundedness, perseverance, and authenticity. Particularly striking, I saw the many occasions, when I was feeling down, discouraged, and spiritually disconnected, I told myself my disempowering story, often using my parents' very words. I saw how each time I told it to myself, I reinforced it. I realized that I have a choice to rewrite this story rather than reinforce it, and that choice requires me to be vigilantly mindful of what I choose to think and to say to myself and others about my life.

The final chapter of the unraveling of this story was the health crisis I related in the preface. At the end of this crisis, as darkness seemed about to overwhelm me, I prayed that if my life and struggles have a purpose, that I be saved from what felt like death itself. Then the dark energy seemed to explode out of me, and I knew that life-affirming healing had occurred. And the dark, deadening story that had played such a key role in my life was gone.

7

SHEDDING OLD SKINS
SO WE MAY GROW

I'd like to begin this chapter by inviting you to go on a journey of the imagination. Relax and imagine . . .

You are in a beautiful, awe-inspiring natural setting—perhaps on a green hillside overlooking a valley or in a desert colored with blooming cactus and multihued rock formations. From your vantage point, you can watch the sun set and brightness slowly give way to twilight. The cares of your everyday life have been left back in the city. Here you feel somehow in touch with the bigger picture—the universal but unique story of growth that has been unfolding through you over the decades. As a bald eagle flies overhead, you feel blessed to be experiencing an eagle's-eye view of your life. Across the screen of your inner awareness pass images of yourself at various stages of your growth— each stage so full of joys, sorrows, opportunities, challenges, strengths, and weaknesses. You are aware that as you sit here, you are at yet another time of transition, of big change. You've been through many transitions before and know how difficult such times can be. However, you realize that this time you are going through transition with more awareness and understanding than ever before. You are experiencing this transition, from identifying as a midlife adult to identifying as someone becoming a conscious elder, with a consciousness and intentionality you have not known previously. As you sit here reveling in the magnificent end to this day, you are feeling both gratitude and trepidation—gratitude for what has been and trepidation at the prospect of leaving behind significant, familiar aspects of who you have been to enter an unfamiliar, unknown future.

As the magenta-streaked sky slowly gives way to darkness and the appearance of the first stars, your nervous anticipation builds, for you know that soon you will approach a sacred fire where you will let go of parts of who you have been. Fire, a powerful primal symbol of transformation, will accept and burn that in you that seeks transformation, which no longer serves your growth. In the burning, energy that has been attached to your old patterns, attitudes, beliefs, behaviors, and self-identifications will be released to serve the new life chapter seeking to emerge in you. You are choosing to use the power of this fire so that, like a snake, you can shed your old skin, which has become too small for the emerging self that your soul envisions for you.

You know that this ceremony is not to be taken lightly. Whether you are about to enact this ceremony alone or with the witness and support of others, you have invoked the presence of the sacred, however you conceive it, to witness and support your ceremony of letting go. You have also invoked the spirits of those you love and the spirits of those in the generations that will follow yours—all of whom will benefit from what you will have to offer the world as you grow into conscious elderhood.

Before you approach the fire of transformation, let's step back from this imagery. I want to share with you my understanding of the role and the process of shedding old skins in becoming a conscious elder. Conscious elderhood is about much more than becoming more intentional about our goals and lifestyle as we seek to prolong middle age for as long as possible. Rather, it is about recognizing, honoring, growing into, and working to embody the role of elder as a distinct life stage full of potential for growth and service beyond midlife adulthood. However, whether we aspire to grow into the role of elder or not, the fact is that if we hope to grow as we age, old skins that no longer fit and no longer serve our well-being must periodically be shed. In acknowledging an elder life stage and role, we become conscious of the many opportunities for inner work that others may not recognize. A critical aspect of this inner work is identifying and letting go of those elements of ourselves and of our lives that keep us bound to the past when the possibilities of the future require clear energy and new vision.

Life review, work with forgiveness, grief work, and the rewriting of disempowering life stories are all facets of the larger process of breaking the hold the past has on us. They are all critical elements of the rite of passage into the role of elder or elder-in-the-making. However, it is important to recognize letting go as a critical process in its own right. Once we have reached a point of being able to forgive, of experiencing and healing old grief, of recontextualizing old experiences and creating new stories, a conscious act of will is required to bring these processes to fruition. As painful or disempowering as elements of our past may have been, they have become part of our sense of identity. It feels safer to associate with what is familiar than to open ourselves to the unknown, yet conscious acts of letting go of what is familiar but disempowering are critical to our growth.

There may be important elements of the things we need to let go of that do not involve forgiveness, old grief, or outworn stories. Rather, what we need to shed may be identification with roles, abilities, or lifestyle elements that brought us satisfaction and served us well in the past but no longer feel alive because their time has passed. It may be that the reality of aging is making it impossible for them to continue to be significant aspects of our lives or just that we find they no longer hold meaning for us as they had. As difficult as it might be to admit, we are growing out of them, and staying attached to them will only turn us into caricatures of our former selves. The process of shedding old skins, even those that have brought us pain, is often painful in itself and accompanied by the grief for significant elements of who we have been. It is important to allow ourselves to acknowledge and feel that grief while anticipating the new optimistic self that is emerging as we move along.

Our intention to let go of elements of who we have been is empowered by our will, but the actual transformation of these beliefs, attitudes, attachments, and behaviors requires more than will; it requires love. It is not possible to free the energy attached to these elements of the past by trying to force them out of ourselves. In attempting to do so, we only empower them as they struggle in our psyches to hold on to their roles in our lives. The harder we try to force them out, the more they resist. The intentional, conscious shedding of old skins is a process that is done gently, with love and gratitude. When we step up to that fire, whether metaphorically or physically, it is essential that we honor and acknowledge the role of what we are shedding in our journey of growth. We express gratitude for what it has taught us and how it has helped shape us into the unique individuals we are. We acknowledge the insight it has provided and the wisdom it has imparted—insight and wisdom we can share with others in our role as elder. Finding such gratitude may be extremely difficult in situations where what we are letting go caused us deep pain. But the fact is that true emotional letting go requires getting to the point where we can acknowledge and honor such experiences as valued teachers. Letting go, with all its many dimensions, is not quick and easy work. It is inner work that takes time and is often done one layer at a time, until we are able to move past the pain and touch the core with the power of our love.

Hanging on to what needs to be shed negatively affects our lives in various ways. It keeps our energy bound to the past instead of allowing it to create the vision and passion we need for the future. The more we resist letting go, the more emotionally numbing it becomes to hold on. If we are not sufficiently aware of what needs to be shed in us and we're not willing to work on letting go, the gentle nudges from our souls grow into serious whacks to the head until we have no choice but to pay attention. Additionally, learning to consciously let go is invaluable preparation for dealing with the inevitable significant losses that accompany aging. These losses send many people into long-term hopelessness and bitterness, but conscious eldering presents another option. As we come to recognize the pain that results from holding on to a past that is no longer possible and experience the new emotional and spiritual energy that results from letting go, we come to see opportunities for growth no matter what we lose. As Ram Dass so beautifully articulates in *Still Here*, the book he wrote after suffering a debilitating stroke, even major loss of physical or mental abilities has the potential to free the spirit in us to shine forth more brightly than ever.[1]

On our conscious eldering retreats, we stress that approaching the ceremonial fire to affirm our willingness to let go is a powerful act that is an exclamation point in an ongoing process. This process may have been going on for some time and may require reaffirmation in the future. We can trust that with intention, commitment, and love, it is indeed possible for us to experience the lightness and aliveness that result from freeing ourselves of constricting old skins as we grow into new, more expansive selves. While participating in an organized ceremonial process is certainly not necessary for doing the work of letting go, such important inner work is strongly supported by employing the power of ritual. Ritual focuses our intention and strengthens our will. It taps the spiritual dimension of ourselves and invests what we do with sacredness. It has the power to open our hearts and minds. It opens us to the transformative fire of love.

You can use your creativity and intuition to create your own rituals for letting go. Prepare by reflecting carefully on what you need to shed. Journal about it. Assess your readiness for letting go. Identify what other work, such as forgiveness or recontextualizing or grieving, may be necessary before you are truly ready to let go. You may want to use ritual to support letting go of several aspects of your past or choose to create a separate ceremony for each one when the time feels right. For many people, it is important to find or create some physical object that symbolizes an old skin to be shed. Spend time with this object, investing it with the energy of what it represents. Before your ceremony, place it in a special place in your home, such as an altar, where it gathers your emotional and spiritual energy for a period of time. On our retreats, participants have burned or buried photos from relationships, certificates of accomplishments in careers that have ended and need to be emotionally released, old letters, journals, pieces of clothing . . . the possibilities are as varied as the individuals involved. One man touched us all deeply when he placed in the fire a worn (and thankfully washed) jock strap, which was for him the most potent symbol of his former strong identification as an athlete. He spoke of the important and fulfilling role his athletic abilities played in his life and then affirmed how, as he ages and loses physical prowess, he needs to let go of his attachment to physical ability while honing his other gifts, such as his abilities as a teacher.

Then when the time feels right for your ritual of letting go, you might build a ceremonial fire into which you place some object that symbolizes what you are shedding. Or you might dig a small "grave" in the earth mother, into which you place such an object if that feels more appropriate to you. Having others present who understand and support you can be empowering and affirming. You might find that you need to speak about what you are shedding to the fire of transformation or to Spirit, however you perceive it. Speak of the significance in your past life of what you are committing to let go. Say why you need to shed it at this time. Allow tears to flow if that's what is needed. Find a way to express gratitude for the contribution it has made to your growth. Then state with strength your intention to let it go, trusting that you are supported in the process of doing so by all those energies and beings you have invited to be present and by that sacred presence within you that is calling you to new beginnings.

Before you return to the imagined ceremony of letting go that resumes below, reflect for a few minutes on something in you or your external life that no longer serves you and needs to be shed. Get in touch with your willingness to let this thing go. Perhaps it is an attitude or a belief. Perhaps it is an old disempowering story, a resentment, a relationship, a job, or some element of your lifestyle. It may be your identification with certain abilities that you need to set aside. Now see yourself sitting in the gathering darkness, with the fire of transformation burning nearby, preparing to approach this fire with love and commitment to your growth.

You know that the time has come to approach the fire. There may be others present or you may be on your own. If others are present, will they also be approaching the fire to let go? You may choose to invoke the spirits of people who are not there in person to witness your ritual. Inviting spiritual energies or presences that have meaning for you can be important. Have you brought some physical symbol of what you are shedding? Now step up to the fire of transformation and offer what you are shedding, speaking your commitment aloud for all witnesses, seen and unseen, to hear as you do so. Are you really ready to let this go, and are you aware of the consequences if you don't release it? Allow yourself to feel a sense of the liberation you hope to experience by letting go.

Once the ceremony is complete, you stand next to the waning fire, in a circle with others if they are present, watching the flames gradually flicker out, leaving only red embers. The firelight gradually gives way to darkness as you stand there, knowing that some aspect of who you have been has died and wondering what new beginnings await you when the time is right. For now, you somehow feel you've taken a step beyond your past toward a vague and mysterious future that is both frightening and inviting. Somewhere in the darkness, an old Buddhist chant begins and you join in: "Gone, gone, gone beyond—gone beyond beyond. All praise to the Spirit within."

STORY BY THE FIRE

Letting Go of My Dream

by Lucia Leck

In 2003 my husband and I were a married couple of thirty-three years and recently retired. We had mutually decided to leave behind our

Chicago-area jobs, home, and community of thirty years to move to northwestern Wisconsin. We moved to our new home in August of that year and christened the place "The Nest," using Letty Cottin Pogrebin's idea that "if a family were a container, it would be a nest, loosely woven, expansive and open at the top, free for comings and goings."[2] We carved "The Nest" into birch bark, made it into a sign, and hung it at the end of the driveway. We mailed announcements with a picture of us standing by the sign, encouraging all family and friends to feel welcome to come and go from our home. Shortly after we moved, we planned a celebratory trip, and we spent Christmas in the Philippines, visiting our youngest child, who was in the Peace Corps. We returned home to "The Nest" February 4. Death came swiftly and surely for my husband there in the early morning hours of February 16.

Shock, numbness, confusion, constant nausea, and a sense of being utterly lost set in. It was impossible for me to travel even well-known roads without the panic of losing my way. I spent days and months looking, searching everywhere and anywhere for something to help me stabilize and ground my world.

In June the opportunity arose to attend an art retreat, during which participants would create spirit houses. The idea was based on an old Southeast Asian tradition that encourages people to build miniature houses that are placed in yards and where the spirits of the land can take shelter and be petitioned to protect the premises. In this workshop, the spin was more on creating a dwelling for one's own individual spirit. I had enough energy to participate and tried to construct a dwelling where my spirit could hole up while I tried to figure out what came next. The spirit house that emerged was in the design and shape of a nest. It was soon placed right under the framed nest picture in the house.

Almost a year later, in March 2005, I learned of an opportunity to participate in a conscious eldering rite of passage. I had never heard of conscious eldering and had very little understanding of rites of passage. The description of what could be expected sounded intriguing and challenging and like something that would put me at the edge of all I thought I knew, just as death had done. I signed up and began the advance preparations laid out for the participants.

By the time June came, all my travel arrangements had been made, and I was packed. The last thing to go in was an object we had been instructed to bring—something that would symbolize the letting go of an old way of being. I packed the nest I had created in the workshop a year ago.

During the days prior to departing into nature for our time of solitude and fasting, we experienced a variety of preparatory activities. One was a fire ceremony. As we sat around the fire, the invitation came for each of us to offer up the object that would symbolize letting go of an old way of life, an old way of thinking and being that would not serve us in our elderhood.

When I was ready, I tossed the nest in. It was an act of profound symbolism with two very different meanings. On one level, it demonstrated my willingness to let go of everything that I had dreamed of for my husband and me in retirement. Nothing could represent that old way of being more than the nest. Burning it was akin to burning my bridges. Now there was no way back to that life. On another level, because there was no life to go back to, death had left me ripe and ready to be filled with the new possibilities of conscious eldering. Death had burned away most everything, but death also opened a door for me to rethink who I was and how I would be in the world.

I gave up being plagued by the question "What are you going to do now?" and replaced it with Rabbi Schachter-Shalomi's words, "Oh my soul, you are growing something special and good inside me. How can I give it the proper sunshine and nourishment to ensure that it grows to health and vigor?"[3] Life was in charge now, and I could only wonder what life was asking of me as I entered more fully into my elder years, alone.

8

RELEASING THE PAST IN
THE DEATH LODGE

When we reflect on our mortality and the passage from this life to whatever comes next, most everyone hopes to die in peace. We want to be able to feel that our lives have been well lived, that we have done our best to use our gifts, that we have loved and been loved, and that we can let go of this life with grace and without regret. Yet so many people do not die this way. Colleagues, friends, and retreat participants who work with hospice say that those who die the most peaceful deaths are usually those who come to their deathbeds unburdened by a lifetime's accumulation of resentments, regrets, dysfunctional relationships, unhealed grief, and closed hearts. Besides manifesting as emotional turmoil, such unfinished business often results in prolonged physical agony, while the dying person clings to a life that feels incomplete and unfulfilled. Often the greatest gift that hospice spiritual directors give to those they tend to is help dealing with unfinished business so that the patients can let go of this life with hearts that are more open to love and peace.

While the conceptions of what comes after this life vary greatly among the world's spiritual traditions, they appear to be unified in their belief that what we carry internally to our deathbeds is critical to what we experience thereafter. In various traditions, heaven and hell are not places but magnified reflections of our inner state at the time of death. Whether we die with peaceful, loving hearts or conflicted closed hearts very much determines our experience when we are without a body. And according to traditions like Hinduism and Tibetan Buddhism that include reincarnation, the extent to which we have healed the past plays a key role in determining our experience when we next inhabit a body.

The work that prepares us to be at peace as we leave this life and step into the great unknown is the same work that prepares us to become conscious elders. It is the work of healing our past and leaving behind our self-identification with our previous life stage so that we can move into the mysterious next chapter that awaits us. Both physical death and the passage into conscious elderhood are, for the psyche, the death of an old way of being. They are also both doorways into new chapters in life's journey of growth. Besides helping to complete unfinished business that ties up our energy, closes our hearts, and dims our vision as we age, this work of healing our past is valuable because it helps us keep our inner work current so that we are ready whenever death calls. When I had my health crisis several years ago, I became acutely aware of healing work I needed to do and legacy stories I needed to share with loved ones. Yet I felt too weak, ill, fearful, and emotionally drained to do any inner work at all. It was all I could do to hang on and keep the myriad of strong emotions that swept over me from turning into overwhelm. That experience taught me the importance of keeping current in my inner work so that I can shine my light brightly in the elder chapters of this life and be ready for the next whenever that time comes.

One of the most deeply healing practices I know for bringing together various aspects of the inner work of healing the past is called the Death Lodge. Because the work of this practice feels so very freeing and enlivening, some of our retreat participants prefer to also call it the Life Lodge. Choose whatever name you prefer. I use the term *Death Lodge* because the work done there is the work of dying to the past to open the door to the future.

I first learned about the Death Lodge many years ago from my teachers Steven Foster and Meredith Little, the pioneers in the modern rite of passage movement. In their book on vision questing, *The Roaring of the Sacred River*, they describe the Death Lodge as "a little house away from the village where people go when they want to tell everyone they are ready to die."[1] Foster and Little attribute the Death Lodge concept to the Cheyenne tribe of the American Plains. When a tribal elder sensed that death was near, he would attend to external practical matters that need to be done at the end of life. Then he would leave village life behind to enter a special place—the Death Lodge—where he would focus on reviewing his life, repairing or completing his relationships, and preparing to move from this life into the mystery beyond.

In today's world, this imagery of a Death Lodge can be a profound catalyst and vehicle for the kinds of inner work that prepare us both for death and for the healing of relationships that is so important in aging consciously. We obviously live in a very different world than the indigenous societies, where the death of the old sense of self that happens at life's major passages is acknowledged and honored as part of the cycle of life and is consciously prepared for. However, deep inside each of us is an archetypal wisdom about how nature's life cycles are also the cycles of our own lives. Conscious eldering is becoming conscious of these rhythms as they operate in us and doing the work at every stage so that the old self can die well and make way for the birth of new possibility. I believe that one reason the Death Lodge practice resonates so deeply with our retreat participants is that its imagery taps into that indigenous knowing in each of us as well as into our understandings of modern depth psychology.

As you employ the Death Lodge to support your passage into conscious elderhood, you are also keeping your inner work current as you draw nearer to life's final passage. As you approach this work, be aware that Death Lodge work is not something you do one time and then it's complete. It is work involving many dimensions of our relationships—with the self, our Creator, the others in our life—and takes time. It is a dynamic practice that can be periodically revisited, and we do some inner work each time we engage it. As we do this work, we can eventually reach a point of feeling we are "up-to-date" in our relationships. For those aspiring to conscious elderhood, Death Lodge work helps prepare us for a beginning as well as an end. It frees up our energy and opens our hearts so that we can live and serve as fully as possible as conscious elders. Then when our physical death arrives, we can pass through that portal as whole beings who have done our work of healing. To use an old Native American expression, it can be a good day to die.

I encourage you to view Death Lodge work as a sacred ritual done with care and intention. If possible, do it outside in a natural place that will help align you with nature's cycles. Give yourself enough time to do focused inner work without distraction. Ideally, find a small area, such as a spot in a grove of trees or a cave-like space amid rocks or under overhanging bushes, that has the feel of an enclosed little house or lodge. Before you enter, offer a prayer or state an intention that the sacred, however you name it, be with you, supporting and guiding your work. You might bless and purify your Lodge with incense or bring in some flowers. Be sure to bring with you your journal and perhaps an object you consider sacred. This work is most profound if you approach it imagining, as best you can, that you have only a few weeks left to live and that you are indeed preparing to die. You never know; that may indeed be the case.

Once inside your Death Lodge, be quiet and wait to see what type of life completion or healing work feels most alive for you. You may choose to bring to your awareness a painful experience that needs to be examined, perhaps felt more deeply, and recontextualized so you can understand how it contributed or can now contribute to your growth. If you are aware of regrets that drag you down and diminish your sense of self-worth, look for ways you might change the way you relate to these regrets. It is valuable and life-affirming to spend time remembering experiences of joy or accomplishment and remembering your strengths and gifts, so I encourage you to spend time focusing on feeling gratitude for the incredible journey that is your life. An important aspect of this work can be devoting time to examining your relationship with the Great Mystery that is your source and essence, however you name and conceive it. Remember how the Great Mystery has manifested in your life in times of joy and in those of challenge. Ask it to be with you as you do your Death Lodge work.

For many people, the most important work of the Death Lodge involves bringing healing and completion to relationships with others. In your Lodge, you have the opportunity to spend time, in spirit, with people who have been significant in your life. When you engage this practice with your mortality in mind, the dynamics of your relationships may well appear quite different than they previously had. Your work is to find what needs to be communicated to bring completion and, if needed, healing to these relationships. If you need to forgive or ask to be forgiven, this is a time to do so. It is a time to remember the contribution the other person has made to your life and growth, even in cases where that contribution has been difficult or painful. The Death Lodge is an opportunity for thanking and honoring those who have been important in your life.

There are several different possibilities for whom you can invite into your Lodge (and sometimes you may find someone knocking at the door without an invitation—a clear indication that they belong there). You may invite in the spirits of those who are alive, with whom healing needs to happen and with whom a face-to-face conversation is possible if you make the effort. Or you may choose to invite in the spirits of those who are alive but with whom a face-to-face meeting is impossible for whatever reasons. The Death Lodge also makes it possible to invite in the spirits of people who have died and with whom you never had the opportunity to share what is in your heart. This can be a wonderful opportunity to find a sense of completion to your relationship with them.

You may also choose to simply sit with your own soul. For many people, the most important and difficult Death Lodge work is the work of forgiving and honoring themselves or, to be more precise, the parts of themselves that have made errors and poor decisions, have hurt others, are weak, and are imperfect.

No matter whom you choose to bring with you to the Death Lodge, the important thing is to start a dialog. You can use your imagination to converse with them, you can speak your thoughts out loud, or you can write in your journal if that will help you more easily imagine a conversation, but be sure to start that conversation because it is essential to resolving unfinished business. In such a conversation, it is important to try speak to the best and wisest part of the person who has joined you in spirit, even if this part is largely unfamiliar to you. Doing so will help ensure that your conversation is as productive and healing as possible.

The hospice tradition has identified four pieces of unfinished business that are important for people seeking peace and wholeness as they near the end of their lives. These four elements can serve as a useful template for the relationship completion work we do in our Death Lodges, and they include:

- Asking for forgiveness from those we have offended
- Forgiving those we need to forgive
- Expressing gratitude toward those who have made a difference in our lives, whether this impact brought happiness or pain at the time
- Saying good-bye[2]

In addition, my dear friend and mentor Wes Burwell, a long-time hospice spiritual director with whom I coguided Choosing Conscious Elderhood retreats over several years, adds a fifth that helps consciously bring the spiritual dimension to this work: Blessing those who have made a difference in our lives.

Death Lodge work is not easy. It requires us to face our mortality and to uncover and deal with difficult dynamics in ourselves and our relationships with others. It is work that is very easily postponed with the rationale that we'll do it later, when we are *really* old and death seems nearer and more tangible. I encourage you to remember these two facts: You don't know when death is near, and the more of this work you do as you age, the more alive, vibrant, inspired, and peaceful you will be in life's elder chapters. The inner work of conscious eldering plays a critical role in determining whether you become merely old or a vibrant, passionate, and ever-growing conscious elder.

STORY BY THE FIRE
From Grief to Gratitude in the Death Lodge
by Anette Edens

There was a moment in time that excruciatingly split my life into the "before" and "after"—the zero on my X-axis of time: June 17, 1999.

The phone rang. A voice said, "Molly has shot herself." She had been at her father's house. In a blur of events I found myself at the emergency room hearing a physician say the words: "She is dead." My daughter was fifteen, brilliant, beautiful, happy, precious, and so very loved by many people. So loved by me. A moment of drama over a boy, an argument with her father, an available loaded pistol, and she gave up every sweetly anticipated experience of growing into adulthood on this earth.

My son, my other daughter, and I lived in a stunned and painful silence, patient and tolerant of each other's grief, absorbing our new reality. A woman from the funeral home brought me a small velvet bag with Molly's jewelry: a watch I had bought her, a silver butterfly pendant on a chain (the symbol of her closest girlfriends), and silver earrings. She had worn these when she died. I held this velvet bag for many months.

Four years later, around Thanksgiving, I began to feel human again, and my son and I remarked that we were smiling.

Twelve years later, a colleague sent me a link to a retreat on conscious eldering that would be held at a small retreat center near

Mount Shasta. We were asked to bring significant objects from our lives—objects that we felt identified us in some way—to create an altar. The thought of Molly, ever-present, kept a lump in my throat and sorrow just slightly beneath the surface. Suicide is different from any other death. There is a stigma. It is impossible to explain, but only other parents of children who have taken their own lives seem to understand the complexity. I took a photo of Molly.

My conscious eldering cohorts were loving, gentle, and experienced in a variety of ways, each bringing a rich perspective to life and life's cycle. I was prepared for my day of solitude and fasting on the mountain and felt content as I approached my little sanctuary. I sprawled on my back to watch the clouds and feel the mountain. It felt safe. It was beautiful. I spoke to a bee. I explored. I came across a circle of stones that had been laid around a small pit. This place, previously created for some sacred moment in another's life, became my Death Lodge. Shasta offered the perfect blending of death and renewal. Felled trees, rotting where they landed, created swells in the landscape, changing the flow of runoff, adjusting the topography, forever changing the landscape by their death. The beauty and symmetry of life amidst decomposition prepared me for my Death Lodge work.

It felt odd to speak aloud to my deceased family members—grandparents, aunts and uncles, and friends who were so dear. There were many I shared this moment with, saving Molly for last. I spoke to my friend Bob, who had shared his death from pancreatic cancer with me just nine months before. As he approached his death, he had said, "Why would I be afraid when I get to fall asleep, relieved of pain, and awaken staring into the eyes of my God?" I thanked him for taking me as far as I could go with him down that path of transforming fear. He gave me, in his death, the ability to see life more clearly. All those who were present for me in my Death Lodge had felt receptive to my gratitude and amends. Now I was ready to speak to Molly.

For the first time in twelve years, I felt her presence. I spoke to her and then with her about my love for her, my horror at her death, and my struggle with the permanence of her choice. I yearned for her to have lived out her life—to have survived that painful moment and to have experienced all that life has to offer—and to find the peace and joy that come from maturity and self-acceptance. I wanted just once more to hear the sound of her voice. I wanted her as the receptacle for immense love and devotion that had welled in my heart with no place to go for so many years. I asked for forgiveness—for what, I do not know. I told her that if I had hurt her, I no longer remembered having done so and wanted her to know that I had to quit trying to figure it out. She understood. Then I heard Bob say, "Why do we dwell on the thought that more is better?" Indeed. I had lived in delight for fifteen years with this precious, clever, beautiful, spontaneous, loving child and yet spent almost all of the following twelve years in pain over her death rather than in awe of her life. I felt the weight lift in an instant. Tears rolling down my cheeks, I pledged to honor her by living in gratitude for her life rather than in misery over her death.

Then a butterfly appeared from the trees and fluttered through the Death Lodge, encircling my head and gracing me with its beauty. As she flew away, I said, "No, come back!" before catching myself in a smile, chuckling at my own compulsion to want more.

From that day, I have loved Molly in joy more than sorrow. My tears are now of gratitude. I miss her terribly, and I am so fortunate to have had her in my life.

9

LIVING IN-BETWEEN: PRACTICES FOR NAVIGATING THE NEUTRAL ZONE

For many of us, the catalyst that makes us aware that we have entered a time of significant inner transition, thrusting us rapidly into the dynamics of both severance and the neutral zone (and for some onto the path of conscious aging), will be retirement. For others, it will be an encounter with mortality, such as illness, or the death or serious illness of someone dear to us. The catalyst may be an undeniable recognition of the diminution or loss of physical or mental abilities. For many, this inner dynamic will be heralded by a subtle recognition that a way of life that was once fulfilling, or at least had served as our identity, is now feeling dull and lifeless. Some of us will bring awareness and intention to the unfolding process and in doing so will lay the groundwork for enlivening new beginnings. A great many others will be unconsciously and erratically carried through the process, experiencing inner turmoil or numbness but not recognizing and claiming the tremendous potential for generating new life after loss.

The transition from midlife adulthood to early elderhood is a passage with powerful internal dynamics. As discussed earlier, any significant passage from one life stage to another, including the passage into conscious elderhood, is a process with three phases or dynamics, which often overlap as we negotiate our passage. These include severance from our previous life stage, navigating the neutral zone, and ending with reincorporation into full engagement with life as we enter our new life stage. In a culture that so strongly values clarity of purpose and direction, for many the neutral zone is the most challenging. We have begun to leave behind aspects of who we have been but are not yet aware of who we are becoming. Whatever the catalyst that pushes us across an internal threshold into this in-between time, once we are there we find ourselves in a mysterious place with few familiar landmarks, many fearsome inner inhabitants, and frequent dark clouds of confusion and hopelessness covering the sun of our optimism.

As difficult as it can be to sever an old identity and aspects of who we have been, for many of us the neutral zone is even more difficult. Loss and letting go are painful, but the unrealistic hope that what we have lost can somehow be quickly replaced can serve to temporarily ease our pain as we experience our loss. But once we enter the neutral zone, feeling stranded between a past that, whether satisfactory or not, was at least tangible and an amorphous future, optimism is hard to come by. We feel lost and alone. This is a time of feeling suspended between an old life and a new beginning. Our sense of having control of our lives is greatly diminished. The neutral zone is not a pleasant place to be. And this is the reason so many of us rush into premature and oftentimes inappropriate and unsuccessful new beginnings rather than facing the discomfort of the neutral zone. We think we can claim the treasures of new beginnings while bypassing the hero's journey.

The world's wisdom traditions understood what the modern world has largely forgotten about human development—that true transformation is always precipitated by an ordeal that has the potential to be an initiation into new life. Virtually every version of the universally recognized hero's journey sees this dark inner place where we confront the dragons of uncertainty, grief, hopelessness, doubt, and seeming loss of control as the place new strength and vision emerge from. In this place, we are confronted with the limitations of our egos and presented with the opportunity to allow the spiritual power and wisdom of our souls to take the lead. It is the place where the alchemy of change awaits us. It is the ground where the seeds of new beginnings must lie dormant through our inner winters until the time is right for germination. The neutral zone is where our old selves decompose to serve as fertilizer for the emergent new life our soul has planted in our psyche, but it can only emerge when inner springtime sheds its light on us.

Whether we are catapulted into the neutral zone or enter through a process that is much less dramatic and traumatic, this is a place of tremendous potential for growth. But the results are by no means guaranteed. Without conscious awareness, it is very possible for you to remain stuck there without a sense of meaning, purpose, or direction, or an understanding of what is happening. You may also try to invest energy in an unfulfilling and inauthentic attempt to recapture a past whose time has ended or create a new chapter that is not yet ready to emerge. Conscious eldering work very much involves crossing the threshold into the neutral zone with awareness of what's going on within and understanding of the dynamics of this critical stage in life transition. It requires courage to confront all that emerges and the skill to make the best possible use of the opportunities afforded by this in-between time. Perhaps most important of all, conscious eldering requires deep trust that life has a plan for our growth and fulfillment and that our journey through the neutral zone is an integral part of that unfolding plan. The deeper our connection with the spiritual dimension in ourselves, the easier it is to access awareness, courage, and trust and skillfully prepare the ground so that the seeds of our potential may eventually produce abundant new life.

As we age, it may well be the case that internally we have entered the neutral zone, while externally our lives look the same as they did before. There may be no clear break with the past to help us let go of our old identity while we yearn for a new one. We may, of necessity or choice, continue working the jobs we have been working, whether they bring us fulfillment or not. We may have to continue meeting certain responsibilities that we would dearly like to shed as we move toward elderhood. The neutral zone is not an all-or-nothing place or state. While it is a strong and often primary inner dynamic at times of transition, it is one we can choose to attend to and work with either intensively or just periodically. We don't have to move into a cave or monastery to undertake this critical work of our hero's journey.

Much of the transformative power of the neutral zone comes from the fact that it is a place of being broken open. When we are firmly entrenched in an identity and a way of life, our egos are generally operating at their strongest. (And remember, we need strong, healthy egos to function in the material world.) We are viewing our lives and the world around us through the limited and conditioned eyes of our ego. However, when life-changing catalysts enter our lives, our egos get broken open or at least cracked. This breaking open has the potential to allow the voice of our soul to enter our awareness. It can give us new eyes and a more expansive view of our lives. It can open hardened hearts and rigid minds. We come to see that our egos, as skillful as they might be, are not sufficient to see us through the challenges of the neutral zone. We need something more, and that something is found in the spiritual depths of ourselves. When we are cracked open, the answers that will provide healing, meaning, and direction can be found not through the efforts of our rational minds but through the language of the deep psyche—the language of soul that speaks to us through intuition, feelings, dreams, synchronicities, and inner stirrings. The neutral zone is often called the liminal time or the liminal world because the language of the deep psyche is so often subtle and not readily perceived by our five senses and our rational minds.

Traditional rites of passage as well as contemporary programs that include the same dynamics are ritualized, highly focused immersions in the hero's journey. However, the inner work of the neutral zone, as is the case with the other two phases, is generally not accomplished in the short time of a structured rite of passage experience. The work of a significant passage often takes months or even years. Life transitions proceed at their own pace and not necessarily in linear fashion. Often the transition process seems to feel like "two steps forward and one step back."

In many traditional and most modern structured rites of passage, after a period of time focused on reviewing and preparing to sever from one's former life and identity, initiates cross a threshold into the liminal world of the neutral zone. Depending upon the format of the experience, this neutral zone time ranges from one to three or four days. On our Choosing Conscious Elderhood retreats, participants spend twenty-four hours away from the community in solitude and silence. Fasting is recommended but optional. In all effective rites of passage, initiates are well prepared for their time across the threshold, having been taught a variety of practices and approaches that can help them open their hearts, minds, and inner senses to the healing, guidance, and transformative power of the Great Mystery they seek to touch and be touched by. However, whether participants engage in a structured rite of passage experience or work to consciously negotiate the neutral zone without structured support, such practices and approaches are powerful tools for the inner work of the neutral zone.

Part of the reason why participants in the Choosing Conscious Elderhood retreats spend those hours away from the group is that the guidance that comes from deep within—those subtle stirrings, images, synchronicities, and that still, small voice within—cannot be perceived amid the noise of daily life. The activities, distractions, people, commitments, physical noise, and mental chatter of everyday life override our soul's subtle promptings. Understanding this, the creators of structured passage experiences throughout recorded history have included times of silence and solitude to help prepare initiates for their next life stages. Jesus Christ and Siddhartha Gautama (the Buddha) both knew of the power of silence and solitude and spent extended time in wilderness away from other people in preparation for embarking on their teaching missions. Consciously navigating the neutral zone requires one to make a commitment to build times of solitude and silence into daily life. Such quiet time will be invaluable, whether it is fifteen minutes each day, an hour a few days a week, or periodic longer blocks of time. Critical to using this quiet time well is acknowledging its specialness as a time for looking within to see and feel what is happening on our passage through inner transition.

Difficult and perhaps turbulent emotions may arise. Even though we have already done some letting go of old identities and the attendant habits, attitudes, beliefs, and emotions that will not serve us on our journeys forward, in the silence and solitude we may become well aware of still more work that needs to be done, of deeper layers of forgiveness or grief work or story rewriting that call for our attention. Areas of our lives that are most in need of healing will likely emerge in our awareness, bringing the painful realization that we can't move forward without attending to them. Important relationships, major regrets, the expression (or lack thereof) of our talents and gifts in the world, or our relationship (or lack thereof) with the spiritual dimension in ourselves may call to be healed. Old grief may emerge. We may feel emotionally numb.

As we tune in to ourselves in the quiet, we may become aware of fear—fear of a future without maps and blueprints; fear of having no future beyond the neutral zone; fear of our inadequacies; fear of the shadow elements in us that need to be faced and owned; fear of having lost control; fear of our true strength and potential; fear of our pain and grief; fear of being afraid. We may have encounters with boredom and feel compelled to look for distraction—any distraction—to provide a sense of being alive rather than facing, learning from, and moving through boredom or numbness.

In times of solitude and quiet, we gain access to the treasures guarded by all these fearsome dragons. This is when we are most likely to experience the stirrings of the new callings and new beginnings that await us. This is when we get a sense of the purpose that calls us and the wholeness that is possible for us. In the inner stillness we feel, perhaps in a more profound way than ever before, the presence of a loving, wise, and guiding force. Moments of great clarity may emerge. We get a sense of the bigger picture unfolding through our lives and of our place in the larger unfolding of life. As we near the end of the neutral zone, we experience the joy of feeling that we will soon cross the threshold back into full emotional engagement with daily life and into a new chapter with vision, purpose, passion, and spiritual support to accompany us.

The most important intention we can bring to our neutral zone work is to be open to whatever we experience; to welcome what arises as an honored guide from the Great Mystery; to resist nothing; and to do our best to touch each moment and each experience with the love that, ultimately, is the force that effects transformation. Some of our neutral zone times of solitude and quiet can be approached with focus and clear intention, when we know how we want to direct our attention and what we want to accomplish. For example, we may decide to do some Death Lodge work, spend time journaling about recent or past experiences, or work on a dream that feels significant. However, I strongly encourage you to approach some of this time with no plan whatsoever—to just be and see what arises. Important messages from within come through "mindless" daydreaming. By just waiting and watching, you may become aware of some specific inner work that feels alive and important in that moment. It is better to just be and wait until something feels alive than to force ourselves to engage in activities that feel more like "shoulds" than true inner callings for attention. I recommend that you bring your journal to all your neutral-zone inner work sessions as a tool to help with your inner work and to capture insights and intuitions, which tend to be ephemeral and easily forgotten.

When engaging in neutral-zone work, try to do as much as possible outdoors and allow the healing, heart-opening power of the natural world to touch and support you. Tapping this power need not require going into the wilderness, although there is great benefit in doing so. It can be as simple as spending time in your garden, in a quiet place in a nearby park, or on a boat on a lake. Wherever you do this work, approaching it as a sacred ceremony empowers it, strengthens your intention, and focuses your energy. It also evokes spiritual presence to support you. You can consecrate your inner work by offering a prayer as you begin or by bringing into your space an object you consider sacred.

I know of no more powerful way to tap the power of solitude and silence than to periodically give oneself the gift of a day in nature—sunrise to sunset—dedicated to doing this neutral-zone work. If you participate in a structured rite of passage, such a day or days in the neutral zone will be built in. If you are not doing this work with structured support, you can create such days for yourself. While any time in the natural world is valuable, creating a day in nature with the intention of having the day be a sacred ceremony that allows you to empower your journey through transition can be invaluable.

Turning a day into a sacred ceremony is best done by spending time beforehand reflecting on your prayers, hopes, and intentions for the day. Before you go out, it is valuable to share them with someone who supports your growth. If you feel unsafe spending a day in nature alone, ask a friend to accompany you and stay somewhere nearby while allowing you solitude and silence. Begin your day with prayer or a simple ceremony to affirm that you are devoting the special day to your growth. Perform a ritual to mark off an area where you will spend most of your time. Many people find it valuable to create a circle of stones or other natural objects, with each object representing a person, living or dead, or a spiritual being you invite to be there with you, witnessing and supporting you. Upon conclusion of your day, share your experiences and insights with the friend who heard your intentions before you went out.

Courting Synchronicity

Psychologist Carl Jung was the first to make the modern world aware of the phenomenon of synchronicity, although courting and understanding synchronicity was integral to the worldview and lives of virtually all indigenous peoples. They experienced a world in which external signs spoke to them about internal phenomena. When they sought understanding of a situation or guidance for how to deal with internal or external challenges, they paid careful attention to happenings in the world around them. They knew that there was a mysterious yet real connection between the psyche and the outer world—that outer conditions provided mirrors to the inner world. They knew that life transitions are times when humans are more open to awareness of these connections and that ritual and ceremony are doorways through which we leave behind ordinary everyday modes of perception and enter that liminal state of consciousness in which these connections can best be perceived.

Of course, it's possible to use our rational minds to try to find connections between outer events and inner experiences. Often such attempts are just mind games, fantasy experiences with no substance. True perception of synchronicity comes from nonlinear consciousness. Its hallmark is a *felt* sense of knowing that an external event is showing us something important to our psyche. It is usually accompanied by a sense of awe or other strong emotion. In trying to describe the experience, the best we can do may be to say, "I just *know* that is an important sign for me." In various indigenous rites of passage, the indicator of a successful time across the threshold was receipt of a psyche-stirring synchronicity. In modern rites of passage experiences, such synchronicities are often the most important experiences initiates tell about upon their return to community.

Synchronicities don't require being in nature to manifest, although being in nature aligns what is most natural in us with the world outside us, helping to catalyze the occurrence of synchronicity as well as opening us to perceive it when it occurs.

One of the most powerful synchronicities of my life happened a few years ago during a difficult neutral zone time. I was conflicted about whether serving as a guide to conscious eldering was the direction I should be taking, as few opportunities to do this work were coming my way even though most of my energy was being devoted to this work. While at my undergraduate alma mater for my daughter's graduation, I went into the college bookstore. Just inside the door was a display featuring the book *Synchronicity* by leadership guru Joseph Jaworski. I had been aware of this book but had never read it. I spent ten minutes browsing through it, felt a strong sense that it had something important to offer me, purchased it, and began to read. A few days later, from out of the blue I received an email from the author inquiring about participation in a Choosing Conscious Elderhood retreat. I had never had any contact whatsoever with him before this email. This experience filled me with awe and made me shiver. It deeply stirred something inside me. (He never did join us on a retreat, but that is irrelevant.) The synchronicity of this event, appearing at a time when I urgently needed guidance and confirmation of my direction as a leader in promoting conscious eldering played an important role in showing me that there is indeed a Great Mystery working with and through my sense of calling.

While there are various theories about how synchronicity works, I know it is real, can be life-transforming, and tends to appear when the psyche is most in need of guidance or the experience of a connection to something larger. Courting synchronicity requires the

intention to shift from ordinary awareness to heightened consciousness and suspension of the rational mind's disbelief. It also requires
a willingness to carefully look to see if the apparent message truly
provides guidance that will empower us on the journey ahead or if
it is merely a feel-good experience or an ego booster. For me, this
means asking if it helps bring out the best of who I am and can be.

Perhaps the most effective way to court synchronicity is to enter
ritual space in whatever way works for you and ask your higher wisdom, however you name it, to give you a sign that will help answer an
urgent question or provide necessary guidance. Then while in that
space of quiet awareness and even after you have returned to normal
life, pay careful attention to all that happens around you, especially
to what external events somehow have an emotional impact. Journaling about such events and their impact can help you understand
such messages that come from both your own deep psyche and the
mysterious greater psyche we are all deeply embedded in.

Learning from Dreams

Dreams are another way that many of us become aware of our inner
life and the guidance it offers. We all dream throughout our lives,
although many of us are unaware of dreaming or are unable to
remember our dreams. The neutral zone is a time when the dream
life becomes amplified for many people—even those who don't usually recall their dreams. Paying attention to dreams at such times can
be immensely valuable in helping us understand the wholeness that
is possible for us and the inner work that needs to be done so that we
may move to the next level of our potential growth.

Humans have always known and honored the power of dreams.
Some indigenous societies considered the dream world to be the

true reality, with the everyday material world a pale or illusory reflection of that greater reality. Among indigenous peoples such as the Rarámuri of Copper Canyon, it is essential that the dreams of the night be told to others each morning, before they are forgotten. It is in the telling that these ephemeral gifts from the spirit become grounded in material reality where they can help bring healing, guidance, and wholeness to everyday life.

Indigenous peoples saw dreams as gifts from the spirit world, whereas modern psychology sees the dream world as a reflection of the workings of the unconscious psyche. However they are viewed, our dreams are valuable sources for understanding the inner (and sometimes outer) dynamics that shape our lives—who we are, who we have have been, and who we have the potential to become. Since becoming increasingly conscious of these dynamics is very much integral to conscious eldering, paying attention to our dreams can be an important aspect of our inner work. The language of the psyche is not the language of the rational, linear, left-brain mind. It is a language of image, metaphor, feeling, and intuition. Dreams are one way (for many of us the most obvious way) our psyches communicate with us.

There are many excellent books and other resources that can help you learn how to understand and benefit from your dreams, and participation in a skillfully facilitated dream group can be invaluable. All these resources stress that the key to remembering dreams is demonstrating to our psyche our commitment to learning from the dreams it gives us. This can be done before we fall asleep by asking for a dream that will help us answer an important question or deal with an urgent situation in our lives, and by having a notebook or audio recorder next to our bed so that when we wake we can write or speak a few details about the dream. In this way these gifts of the night are not lost as we enter daytime consciousness.

My colleagues and I have found a few general principles that are useful in helping people learn from the dreams that are evoked by the life transition process. Perhaps most important is to recognize that dreams are energized images that are better experienced than interpreted. If you have a dream, especially one with a strong emotional charge, rather than rushing to interpret it, carry it with you as an object of meditation. Tell the dream to someone who supports your growth. Insight often arises just from the sharing. Periodically revisit the dream. Get deeply relaxed and try to relive the dream, feeling the emotions and seeing if the dream wants to further unfold. As you carry the dream, ask your inner wisdom (however you perceive and name it) for clues to help you understand the message in the dream. These clues might come in the form of insights or even synchronicities and might come days after you have the dream.

There are various types of dreams, reflecting various depths of the psyche and potential for growth. At the surface level, many of the dreams we have in our regular daily lives are the result of our psyches processing daily experiences. At a deeper level, many dreams, and especially dreams of the neutral zone, are reflections of inner dynamics being brought to our attention so we may better understand and consciously work with these parts of ourselves. Some dreams show us aspects of people or events external to us, helping us understand our relationship to them. In some dreams, we experience fear, pain, or other emotions that are not ours alone but rather those of the world around us, reflections of our connection to the community of humanity and all living beings. There are anecdotal stories of large numbers of people having unusual nightmares in the days before traumatic events such as 9-11 and the Japanese earthquake and tsunami of 2011. Then there are the huge archetypal dreams that come to some of us in moments of grace where we feel touched by the Great Mystery itself and are in some way forever changed. Such dreams need no interpretation. We know throughout our being how they have impacted us.

Given the mystery and complexity of the dream world and the fact that dreams can blend together several of these possibilities, there is no fast and easy technique for understanding dreams. There are many different approaches to dream work, which reflect the fact that working with dreams is more an art than a science. Given this diversity, there seems to be general agreement that each of our psyches is unique, developing throughout life its own images and symbols, based upon our unique set of experiences. For this reason, dictionaries of dream images are of limited value. While some teachers stress that there is value in working with any dream we remember, most of us who remember many dreams don't have the time to do so. In my experience, for people like me whose dream life is very full, dreams with a strong emotional charge are the ones with the most to offer as we work with them. The emotional charge may well be the psyche telling us to pay special attention. On the other hand, for people who seldom remember dreams, remembering any dream is unusual and deserves attention. The process described below for working with dreams is the one my colleagues and I find to be of the greatest general value for our retreat participants. I encourage you to try it, keeping in mind that it may not be useful for every dream. Don't rush to conclusions about your dreams, even when working with them seems to provide insight. Carry them with you. Try to live into them. Allow them to do their work on you as you bring your awareness to them, and you may find that their message to you becomes clearer and deeper over time.

The general understanding we bring to this approach is that every element of the dream is a reflection of some aspect of your own psyche. The dream is showing you some aspect of the dynamics that lie beneath your conscious awareness and have much power over your life.

When you awaken in the morning or during the night, it is important to somehow capture on paper or audio recorder enough of the dream that you don't lose it as soon as you become active. First, write the dream (or tell the dream to someone who really cares) in the present tense. This helps make the dream more immediate so that you are, in a sense, experiencing it again rather than merely recounting it. Then write (or tell) the dream again, this time acknowledging every element in the dream as a part of yourself. It is understood that "you" in the dream are your ego self as you experience yourself in everyday life. Here's an example: "I am in the desert (of myself) walking down a deep canyon (of myself.) My walk is peaceful until I hear a rustle in the thick brush (of myself), and when I turn to look, see a large mountain lion (of myself) only several yards away. At first I am terrified and want to run, but I remember that running is the most dangerous thing I could do. As I stand there in terror, with the lion (of myself) just looking at me, a white-haired elder woman (of myself) appears around a bend in this canyon (of myself). This elder woman (of myself) approaches me and tells me . . ."

After this second writing or telling, reflect on what the key images in the dream represent to you. What associations do you have with the desert and what might the desert in you be? What in you might a mountain lion represent? What is the elder woman in you? You might also try to start a dialog, perhaps using your journal, with the key images from your dream. You may be surprised at how such dialogs begin to have life and feel real, providing insight not normally accessible to your rational mind.

If you find that your dream has provided guidance of some sort, look for a way to apply that guidance in your life in a tangible way as soon as possible. This can mean creating some simple ritual to acknowledge the guidance or setting an intention for some inner change or outer action.

Creative Expression

Our rational linear thinking capacities play critical roles in helping us live as effective human beings. They are the capacities most valued by modern society, often to the exclusion of our intuitive, imaginative, emotional, and kinesthetic ways of knowing. In times of transition, rational thinking alone will not be sufficient to enable us to be aware of our changing inner landscape and the call to growth that comes from within. We may create lists of pros and cons, strengths and weaknesses, options and closed doors, and there is value in doing so. But ultimately the passage from life stage to life stage is about our soul calling us to our next stage of growth and the inner realignment necessary for that to unfold. Try as some may to avoid this reality, the neutral zone plunges us into a different world requiring different modes of perception.

Any form of creative expression we resonate with is especially valuable during such times when inner sterility and lack of purpose and passion may be frequent visitors. Creating works of art, engaging in creative storytelling, writing poetry, trying to bring creativity to our music making, finding playful ways to express ourselves—all these activities and many more can be instrumental in helping to get our intuition and inspiration flowing and free up stagnant energy. In the neutral zone, creative expression can be seen as more than merely a diversion to help us feel better. It can be a powerful practice that supports our journey toward seeing our new beginnings. A valuable practice for stimulating insight about questions we carry or directions to take, an application of basic principles of creativity theory, is to first spend some time engaged in rational thinking or writing about a particular challenge, possibility, situation, or course of action you are facing. Then let that go and engage in a creative activity you love. The rational thinking can help prime the pump so that the creative activity then opens up other creative or intuitive modes of perceiving the situation.

Strengthening Your Spiritual Connection

We are multidimensional beings whose wholeness depends upon integration of body, mind, emotions, and spirit. The spiritual dimension of ourselves—our soul—is the source of our glimpse of the big picture in which we each have a critical role. Experience of the spiritual dimension is where we know, in a way that feels much more profound than conceptual knowing, the interrelationship of all of life. It is also where we understand our unique calling to use our gifts in service of that greater whole. That spiritual dimension is the source of the deep passion, peace, and sense of purpose (even in the face of loss and adversity) in conscious elders that often seems to defy expectation and explanation.

With much of the inner work of conscious eldering centered around life review, healing the past, and wandering without maps in the neutral zone, the strength of our spiritual connection becomes critically important. Those deeply spiritual moments of knowing are what keep our inner fires alive in our darkest times. Indeed, the strength of our spiritual connection is critical to our transitions fully meeting their potential. These passages between life stages require us to choose to let go of the past in ways that feel like death to our ego and to enter that strange neutral zone where our ego has little to offer us other than resistance. If our ego cannot provide the deep healing of the past and the soul-stirring sense of purpose for the future that we yearn for in the neutral zone, what is there to see us through our transitions other than our spiritual selves? This is why the most important work of conscious eldering, and especially of our times in the neutral zone, is to expand our consciousness of our spiritual dimension.

Those who feel called to conscious eldering generally already have some understanding of what paths and practices best help us tap the guidance and power of spirit. Our journey onto this path requires us to commit to deepening our spiritual lives, using whatever practices most resonate with us. What is essential is that these beliefs and practices support the deepening of our compassion for *all* beings and our commitment to becoming whole as elders so that from that wholeness we may serve the greater whole. Just remember that regardless of what spiritual path you choose, the journey to the depths of your soul is greatly facilitated by nurturing your felt sense of deep relationship with the natural world.

STORY BY THE FIRE
Snakes and Synchronicity in the Neutral Zone
by Diane Allan

As I was out walking on the first morning of the retreat in New Mexico, I spotted a rattlesnake beside my foot, camouflaged in the grass and shadows. I stopped dead, frightened and awestruck by seeing something so powerful so close. It was groggy from the cool temperature, so it did not coil to strike as I sidestepped away. It set an instant tone and edge to my awareness. We had been warned that rattlesnakes were just emerging from their dens and to be cautious but also assured that the risk of seeing one was small if we were attentive to everything around us.

On a warm, sunny afternoon a couple of days later, we were sent onto the land to reflect upon our legacy, to consider what were the most important aspects of our lives we wished to share with our family. I just wanted to play, so I was having a really hard time attending to this agenda. I walked south, quite far from the retreat center, across a creek bed to a very large and intriguing earth mound. I was really enjoying the freedom and openness of the land and celebrating my deep connection to the earth. I even howled like a coyote a couple of times. It was just such a powerfully alive, fun afternoon. Eventually, I began heading back toward the retreat house when I came across another rattlesnake, much larger than the first. It, too, just lay there, unmoving, partially hidden between the rocks and tall grasses. I quietly watched it. Suddenly it coiled and rattled sharply, preparing to strike, and I realized my dangerous position. I stood statue-still while it rattled and hummed. Eventually, it no longer felt at risk and slid away.

An incredible fear rose up through me, and I collapsed, shattered into pieces. I was physically immobilized, sobbing, and fearful of more snakes. It seemed I was miles away from the retreat house (though in reality I was maybe one mile away), and I couldn't imagine how I would ever get back there alive. I found a stick and poked it in the grasses far in front of where I walked, just step by step, inch by inch, sobbing the whole way. I had to go back across the creek bed and slowly make my way back to the house. Unable to pull myself together to join the group, I lay howling on the ground.

I was in total despair, my thoughts jumbled and jagged. Things like, "Oh my God, I could have died," which led to, "It wouldn't have mattered three months ago, but now it does." And, "The last ten years of my life have been a total waste." And, "If I am not working, then my life has no direction, but I know I am really done with social work. How do I go forward?"

This was an existential crisis and too much to hold. The encounter with the snake shocked me into my new reality. I had been confronted by the possibility of my own death, and I felt as if I had not yet even lived. My life had been mainly focused upon work; I had been successful and honored in my field. But if I weren't a social worker, then what? Then who? Now there was time to figure that out and I was completely terrified. After Ron and Anne mopped me up, I was able to hear the truth that the only barrier to being the person I wanted to be was me.

In various indigenous cultures, snakes symbolize transformation, opening new dimensions and levels of awareness, health, and creativity. I had become unconscious and had been taking my life for granted. The encounters with snakes were wake-up calls, and I was forced to confront old beliefs and how I was living my life. Life would no longer be the same, and I needed to forge a new path forward, step by step.

A couple of days later, as I left the group to begin my time of solitude, I was frightened but determined. Anne coached me on doing a ceremony to begin my solo trek that included calling on the energy of the snake and asking its guidance and protection while also asking that it not appear physically. It was important to respect that this was a powerful symbol for me at this time and to develop a healthy relationship with this energy. Snakes did not appear, and my solo was a deeply meaningful time when I let go of my disappointment in myself and started to rewrite my demoralizing stories about the previous decade. I let go of old dreams so that I could pursue new ones.

Approximately ten months have passed since attending the retreat. It has been a time of resting, walking, journaling, connecting with friends, and just allowing myself to feel lost and confused as I continue to move through this neutral zone in my transition into elderhood. It doesn't take a snake ten or more months to shed its skin, but it seems to have taken me that long for the new version of myself to cautiously flow into place. My goal for the retreat was to immediately find and get going with a new life purpose—a very ego-oriented approach. Now I am patiently and gradually learning much more about who and what I am—a multifaceted person with many interests and a good friend to others. As yet I have no clear direction, and this is good! My present purpose is to really value my life as I learn to live it consciously and with gratitude in the present. I am exploring my creativity through writing and art journaling, and I have strongly focused on improving my physical health through changes in diet and exercise. I do more of "nothing" and highly value this time for personal reflection. My life has become one of "being" rather than one of "doing."

10

SERVING AND SAVORING
AS WE AGE

A wonderful diversity of people attend the workshops and retreats offered by my organization and others committed to helping support the development of conscious elders. Those who attend may be just approaching elderhood or well into it, and they bring with them a vast array of perspectives, needs, and vision for the future. This diversity certainly reflects the reality that the ways people claim the role of elder are as varied as the people aspiring to that role. However, there is a common theme echoed by nearly all those called to this exploration: the need to be of service to something larger than themselves and to use their gifts, skills, and wisdom developed over many decades to make a real difference in this world. These are people who believe they have a lot of legacy-building yet to do, and they are committed to finding ways to do it. At the same time, in this life stage

131

they want to honor their inner call to reflection, inner growth, savoring life, and focusing more on *being* and less on *doing*. Learning how to balance these needs is a critical task for the conscious elder.

It is natural for the earlier stages of our lives to be heavily focused on doing. We learn much about who we are and what we are capable of by acting in this world. It is through doing that we develop a strong, effective ego and use that ego in service to our career, relationships, and sense of fulfillment. At the same time we also learn much about how others expect us to be. Most of us have internalized these expectations, having learned how to act effectively in the world but losing awareness of our authentic uniqueness in the process. One of the significant shifts that occurs as we age and become increasingly aware of our mortality is an inner call to focus more on who we are as unique beings and how we let this shine through our lives. In other words, we focus on how we will *be* as we engage in activity and feel less defined by what we will *do*.

In later elderhood, this inner movement strongly calls us to cultivate our inner life, simplify our outer life, and savor each moment and experience with gratitude. As we do so, what is most authentic and soul-infused in us has the opportunity to shine forth more brightly than ever and touch those around us, whether we are doing much or little. In earlier elderhood, we begin to feel this same prompting to quiet and inner focus, but we may also feel strongly called to action, to finding effective ways of using our gifts to serve the community in the role of elder. Seeking balance between serving and savoring, doing and being, conscious elders become increasingly able to have our doing be in service to our souls and to the greater universal spirit rather than to our ego's needs.

In my own conscious eldering, I am facing a challenge that confronts many people who recognize the importance of their contributions as elders to a world in need. I am passionately committed to having my Center for Conscious Eldering be a significant force for transformation, and there is a strong tendency in me to approach my work at the age of sixty-five in the same driven way I approached projects when in my thirties, forties, and even fifties. There were many times then when I lost touch with my joy and inner balance as I pushed ahead. For that time in my midlife adulthood, such an approach may have been totally appropriate. I needed to learn to push beyond my perceived limits and learn something critical about my drive and passion. That was a time of building a strong, effective ego that could succeed in the world.

Now my growth requires something else. It requires learning to allow my soul and its energies to work through my personality as I give my best to my calling, rather than believing that my personality self has to do it all. I see that I am effective only when I am living and working from my wholeness, balancing the needs of my body, mind, emotions, relationships, and spirit. When I allow myself to get out of balance, my work begins to feel not like my calling but like a big de-energizing "should," and my work and I suffer for that. Conscious elders are not martyrs. Older people who become martyrs are not acting with consciousness. When our call to service becomes a "should" or an exercise in ego rather than a balanced outflowing from our hearts, we run the risk of having it be compromised by the untransformed shadow elements in us that must be dealt with if we are to bring wholeness to our service. As I recognize my changing needs at this stage of my life, this means that I may quantitatively accomplish less with my organization than I might prefer. But paradoxically, what I do accomplish will have a greater impact than would be the case if I did more, because I am aligning my actions with the power of my soul.

Another factor in this equation of balance is the tendency many of us have as we age to believe that we are no longer capable of making a difference or that seeking pleasure or focusing only on ourselves after a lifetime of hard work is our much-deserved primary goal in our aging. The danger in this is that we fool ourselves into living a life where our potential for fully being ourselves as we serve the greater whole is greatly truncated. We think we are serving ourselves when we are actually diminishing ourselves. Any worthy endeavor, including service as elders, requires work, effort, and some sacrifice. It requires stretching ourselves regularly rather than allowing the muscles of our intentionality, flexibility, and will to atrophy. It's a question of finding balance and living from wholeness.

Learning this changing balance as our bodies, energies, and psyches change throughout our elder chapters is key to our conscious eldering, especially as we enter the latter stages of our elderhood, when we may well experience partial or complete loss of ability to be physically or mentally active. This does not mean that our service to the world is over. Our inner work of conscious eldering is what can prepare us to gracefully (albeit with the grief of loss) let go of our identification with our bodies, minds, and emotions, as we have done with other identifications throughout our lives. When we can do this, our inner light is freed to shine through more brightly than ever, becoming a source of healing and inspiration for others. What more important gift can we give than continuing to serve the community through the power of our consciousness in the final stages of our elderhood?

As I write this, in my mind's eye I see my dear friend Robert, a brilliant man who had an illustrious career as a scholar and teacher. For decades Robert devoted himself to cultivating his inner life. Now in his later elderhood, Robert is experiencing a huge shift. The mental abilities that served him so well are giving way to an inner joy and radiance that deeply touches those who spend time with him. He reminds me of the aspen trees in his beloved New Mexico, which in autumn cease producing the chlorophyll that gives their quaking leaves a shimmering green color throughout summer. As the chlorophyll decomposes and the green is lost, the brilliant hues of yellow and gold that are masked by the chlorophyll come to the forefront, producing incredible fall beauty. Robert and his wife, Elizabeth, both powerful models of true conscious eldering, are approaching his cognitive decline as yet another spiritual journey to be honored for its potential to allow his soul to shine through. Robert can no longer *do* as he once could, and awareness of this brings him pain at times, but his *being* is a true gift to others.

The archetypal role of elder is indeed one of service to community, but it is a service that flows naturally from wholeness rather than a set of "shoulds." The work of conscious eldering is very much about approaching our elder years with intentionality grounded in our own unique sense of knowing how we can move toward wholeness. Our extended rite of passage from midlife adulthood through the neutral zone into our elder chapters begins to get us in touch with this knowing, giving us glimpses of what is possible for us and what steps we can take to actualize these possibilities in early elderhood and the years beyond. As we get more and more in touch with our souls during our passage, we become aware of those goals and actions that are right for us and deserve our intentionality.

I know many people in their late fifties, sixties, seventies, and even eighties who lead very active lifestyles. Many of them are retired; some retired well before the standard retirement age of sixty-five. I so often hear them say, in one way or other, that they do this sporting activity or that volunteer work in order to "have something to do, something to keep busy." This is such a contrast to those who come to conscious eldering retreats and workshops who speak of their passion for making a difference, and having their lives be an expression of a deep (although often ill-defined) sense of calling. There is a big difference between filling time and trying to live one's precious elderhood with as much purpose and passion as possible. I realize that when I write about such distinctions, I run the risk of appearing—even being—judgmental. My dedication to conscious eldering is a commitment to helping increase awareness of a new, more empowering, purposeful, intentional, and passion-driven vision of what our elder years can be. An increasing number of people in their late fifties and beyond resonate with this way of life, but I honor those who do not embrace this vision. I strive to increase their awareness of what is possible. How to age is a choice. My goal is to help others see that we do have choice in our aging and that our choices have consequences for ourselves and for our descendants, who will look back upon us as their ancestors and wonder what we did to help assure a healthy world for them.

Becoming increasingly conscious of what we can contribute, of that place where the world's needs best intersect with our deepest, passion-filled calling, is a primary goal of the journey of conscious eldering. It's not the only goal, but the more conscious we become, the more we realize that it is necessary for the fulfillment of our other goals. We see that our inner peace and continuing growth cannot be accomplished in isolation. Our well-being is inextricably linked to the well-being of the larger community. Becoming conscious of our inner guidance and what it shows us about how we can best serve as elders is a result of the inner work detailed in this book. This clarity and passion is the result of intentionally working with our psyche to move through the neutral zone into the new life stage of elderhood.

For many of us, it is tempting to try to skip past the often-difficult inner work as we try to chart a course for our elder years. There are many books and resources that can help us become more aware of our talents and passions and then become more intentional with them. However, by jumping to this step of trying to define and pursue new beginnings without first dealing with endings and negotiating the seemingly empty yet fertile space of the neutral zone, we do ourselves a disservice. We act out the modern world's paradigm of trying to have it all now, without regard to the natural rhythms of inner life. We tell ourselves we can reap the rewards of the hero's journey without having the courage to take that journey. The result, in terms of our personal fulfillment and ability to contribute our best, may well be much less than what is possible. It's up to you to decide whether "good enough" is good enough for you as you age.

If you do decide to embark on a journey of conscious eldering, as you near the end of the neutral zone and approach the new beginnings of the phase of reincorporation, you will likely be blessed with precious glimpses of what is possible for you. But even as you get glimpses of how you can best serve others while serving your own growth, you may face challenges requiring the best of your consciousness and courage. Foremost among these may be fear of taking action on a vision that stirs you when you do not yet see a clear path ahead or do not even see more than vague intimations of what you are being called to. Perhaps your obstacle is not so much fear as inertia. Perhaps it is old disempowering beliefs (that need to be examined and shed) about what you are capable of. Perhaps it is a sense of conflict between that vision of service and other goals. Whatever the case, it is essential that you act on strong inner stirrings, trusting that one step, however small, will lead to awareness of your next step and then the next one. This takes courage, as does every aspect of conscious eldering. By not acting, however, you risk paying a big price. The energy of your passion becomes toxic to your being when you hold it inside rather than acting on it.

When you receive a soul-stirring glimpse of how you can best serve, even a first step may be difficult to see. You may feel called to try to make a difference in an area where you see little if any models, structures, institutions, or other support. But this is how so many of those ideas and projects that make a real difference get started. I firmly believe that our soul does not give us callings that are impossible to achieve in some way or other. Your task as a conscious elder is to bring the best of your courage and creativity to the callings you feel, continually reaching deep inside for guidance and strength, and reaching broadly outside to find people and opportunities to align with as you work, step by step, to bring your gifts to the world. In the transition process, resources such as life coaches, skills inventories, and books on encore careers or finding purpose after retirement can be of greater value for us once we have done neutral zone work and begin to glimpse new beginnings and new growth, than before these stirrings arise from within. In this process, resources are not being used as substitutes for doing our inner work but as valuable complements to it.

But these struggles to see the path in front of us are not always the only things preventing us from following our callings as conscious elders. Especially in today's struggling economy, I have heard many people speak of how much they wish they could begin to see themselves in the role of elder, doing what they feel passion for, but the reality is that they must earn a living by whatever means they can find. They tell me that conscious eldering seems like a luxury for the well-off and something with little relation to their own lives. This is indeed a huge challenge for many people who feel trapped between a lifestyle that brings little fulfillment and a vision of a way of aging that seems impossible for them. I'd like to address this concern in two ways.

Service to others as a conscious elder is not defined by how big or visible our actions are. Rather, it is defined by the consciousness and love we bring to whatever we do. We all know people holding seemingly humble jobs who are inspirations to others. There's something about them we want to be around. They may not find their work fulfilling, but they bring a quality of presence to it that somehow transforms it and themselves. They are shining lights in the darkness. In addition to doing their inner work of eldering, those required to do unfulfilling outer work in their elder years can greatly benefit from finding some form of expression for their gifts and sense of calling— something that brings them alive. Whether it is volunteer work, an avocation, a hobby, or spending special time serving as mentor to a young person, the form is not nearly as important as the intention behind it. For many, bringing the best of their love and consciousness to grandparenting is a beautiful, life-enhancing expression of elderhood. Conscious elderhood is about doing our best to grow and serve in whatever role life places us in. We disempower ourselves by believing that we would pursue conscious eldering if only our lives were different in this way or that. The world needs elders who bring consciousness and intention to whatever they do, in whatever circumstance they find themselves.

There is yet another dimension to this discussion, however. Many people trade fulfillment for security. We all know that much of what we consider necessary really isn't. Many of us make a choice, often with little awareness of doing so, to value material possessions over inner growth and fulfillment. That choice is certainly an understandable reflection of the values of the mainstream culture we are embedded in. A significant dimension of conscious eldering is becoming aware of the choices we make and the forces at play as we choose. As our awareness increases, many of us will find that it is more important for us to grow, serve, and be fulfilled than to have some of the things we previously believed to be important. Our sense of security need not be entirely dependent on our material well-being, and many come to find that their conscious elderhood is at least as important to their sense of well-being as the amount in their IRA. The path of growth is indeed a hero's journey rather than a luxury for those with time and money on their hands. It requires us to continually make choices about what is most important to us and to become aware of the values that drive the choices we make.

STORY BY THE FIRE
A Community Discovering Our Elderhood
by Susan Prince

What does it mean to be an elder? I was first presented with this inquiry at the age of fifty-five. I was just beginning to feel resistance to our society's concept of being older, and the word "elder" felt uncomfortable and weighty. However, "elder" also can demark respect—a carrier of wisdom—so I questioned whether I was even close to an age venerable enough to embody elderhood.

I had become part of a group of people working with Jon Young, a cultural anthropologist and longtime student of Native American culture who was exploring what it would be like to live in a community based on the traditional indigenous ways in our region of California. The goal was to create a lineage of mentors who could bring nature awareness into the larger society. We would encourage young people to take their lead from their environment—learning intuitively, as humans have done for the majority of our time on this planet. But in order to foster this type of mentoring, Jon saw that there was a clear need for elders who could hold the role of wisdom keepers and cultural anchors.

The most challenging thing about becoming elders in modern Western culture is that we have few models. Some of us can remember a wise and supportive grandparent or older family friend who was there for us, but in this time of fractured family units and nomadic societies, most of us have grown up without elders. So if we agree that growing into the role of elder is a good thing, then the next step is to decide what that is going to look like in our modern world. This has been a challenge. Many of us in our group found it difficult to follow the traditions of the Haudenosaunee nation. Our group of aspiring elders didn't have anything resembling a traditional longhouse to gather in on a regular basis. In fact, we rarely were together in the same physical space, and our community was dispersed throughout the Bay Area and beyond. And not all of us were comfortable doing Native American ceremonies and working with an indigenous model we had difficulty relating to.

But as we spent more time together in community, attending ceremonies, meetings, gatherings, and workshops as we sought to understand what elderhood could mean for us, we slowly realized that something had been growing organically. Almost ten years have passed since we started, and after showing up time and again to listen to the young people and to hold each other with Peacemaking Principles as our guide, we have discovered that we are now acting as elders.

What has become clear to me over this process is that our culture needs embodied elders. The children and young people need grandmothers and grandfathers, and the middle-aged folk need aunts and uncles. They need us to be the placeholders in a world that is increasingly speeding up, and we need them to count on us to be that calm presence in the midst. This role is one that I have come to value immensely. Now at sixty-five, I recognize the responsibility inherent in being this age, and it's work that I welcome wholeheartedly. Being part of a community of elders gives me the support I need.

11

CONSCIOUSLY BUILDING
LEGACY

Six years ago, when I had my first encounter with my mortality, the theme of legacy was acutely present for me. This awareness took two forms. One was the realization that much stronger than fear of death was my fear of dying without having fulfilled my potential for developing and using my gifts to help create a healthy, life-supporting world for my descendants. The other was the realization that if I were to die soon, my children, both in their early twenties, would never truly know who their father was. It felt very important to me that they (and their children and the generations to follow) know the values, challenges, inner strengths, and sense of calling that most strongly defined this father, grandfather, and ancestor named Ron. Communicating these things is part of the legacy I dearly want to leave them.

We all create a legacy, consciously or not, and these legacies are a mixture of positive and negative elements. The word *legacy* can be defined in various ways. Perhaps most simply, legacy is how we will be remembered—the mark we make on the world, for better or worse. A more complete and nuanced definition of legacy focuses on the impact we have made on others as we have touched their lives, either directly or indirectly. Working to gain conscious awareness of the legacy you have created up until this point in your life is a key dynamic in conscious eldering, and cultivating this awareness is an important element of life review work. Such awareness helps you recognize attitudes and behaviors that have not supported your well-being or that of others. It enables you to cast off those attitudes and behaviors as you move into elderhood. It also provides you with the opportunity to work to repair relationships, make necessary amends, and take other steps to transform any negative elements of your legacy. Of equal importance, this awareness helps you identify the positive life-supporting qualities you can use as the foundation for a new life chapter and the legacy you can create in this emerging chapter. Cultivating awareness of legacy is important in growing the story of who you have been, with your flaws and strengths, into an empowering one that will help bring out the best in you as you grow into elderhood.

One of the huge flaws in the current way aging is viewed in our society is that legacy building is seen as being pretty much over by the time we reach retirement age. This disempowering view holds that whatever legacy will define our lives has been created in our "productive" years, with the years after that being an opportunity to rest on our laurels (if we see our legacy as having been positive.) However, those who seek a conscious elderhood are not willing to allow the twenty or thirty years of life after retirement to be seen as merely the postscript to a legacy created in earlier chapters. Conscious elderhood sees the elder years as the time when legacy can come to true fruition—when the positive personal qualities developed over decades can reach their fullest expression and when a treasure trove of life experience can be converted into the wisdom that only the passage of many years combined with inner awareness can bring. As a conscious elder, you have the opportunity to build on the legacy you have created so far and a chance to create an even fuller and more life-supporting legacy to hand down to the generations that will follow.

To do this, you must begin by working with the legacy you have already created. One of the most powerful practices I know for increasing awareness of our legacy to date is the creation of what we on our retreats call a legacy letter. Some refer to it as an ethical will. A legacy letter can be viewed as a self-created eulogy for the person you have been up to this point. It is a way for you to honor your unique life story, filled with success and failure, joy and sorrow, strength and weakness, and, above all, growth, and to share this story with those who follow you.

While lying in that hospital bed, I felt a strong need to create such a letter for my children. Sure, my children know me in some important ways. They have experienced me as a mostly loving, supportive, and responsible father committed to making a difference in this world. They know some of my strengths and weaknesses. But there's so much they don't know. These are not things that children can understand, even if they are told. Their children (our daughter has just given birth to our first grandchild) will know even less about my life, and these children's children will know me only as someone in family photos and videos. A legacy letter is a precious gift to our descendants, and its creation is an important gift to ourselves. As we work to become increasingly conscious elders, our letters can take many forms and range in length from a page or two to many pages, complete with photos.

If you choose to write such a letter as part of your conscious eldering work, begin by doing your best to imagine that you have only a limited time to live—perhaps one month or six months. This gives a sense of poignancy and urgency to your writing. Then try to get a sense of who you are writing this letter for (besides yourself), as this can help move this process from the realm of abstraction to an emotion-infused reality. You might write your legacy letter with a specific grandchild or grandchildren in mind or address it to some other child who is important in your life. Or you might write to future descendants several generations removed. Once you feel your letter is complete, you can decide how and when to make it available to whomever it is addressed, knowing that you can add to it later or in the future create an addendum that reflects the legacy of your elderhood. It is often the case that children or grandchildren who are too young or have no interest in reading such a letter at this time will find it a precious gift further down the road.

A legacy letter differs from a typical eulogy in that it's not just a recitation of your positive qualities. It differs from some definitions of an ethical will in that it is not just a listing of values you want to communicate. It is not merely a family history, although elements of that can be woven in. Rather, it is an opportunity to paint a verbal picture for your descendants of who you—their ancestor—were. Think about what you would most like them to know about your life: events and people that played the most significant roles in shaping who you became; your biggest challenges and weaknesses and how you dealt with them; key turning points; your most dearly held values; your spirituality; the personal qualities and skills that helped define you as the unique person you have been.

A legacy letter is not something to be done in one sitting; rather, it is an unfolding project that is best seen as a piece of your ongoing inner work to heal and honor your past as your unique expression of the universal hero's journey of growth. As you do your inner work, your awareness of what can best go into your legacy letter will grow, as well as your realization that this letter and the legacy it communicates will not be truly complete until an important new chapter of your life—your elderhood—is over. Hopefully, there will be much to add as the years go by. For now, it tells of the life of someone (you) who is entering an important life-changing passage and seeking to mark it consciously.

In addition to writing a legacy letter, I encourage you to consider creating an oral history video of yourself and for others in your community. Doing video-based oral history work with my parents and other relatives and then with seniors in our community was a major catalyst for my exploration of conscious eldering, both personally and professionally. Through my interviews with these people, I came to recognize their richness of experience, skill, and, in many cases, wisdom. I saw inner strength that carried them through huge life challenges. In many of them I saw great dignity forged in the fires of living and growing. While hesitant at first, most of them quickly opened up to me and became engrossed in telling their stories. For many, this was the first time anyone had given them full attention, asking them about their values, life challenges, significant learnings, joys, and sorrows. I loved doing this oral history work, seeing how healing it seemed to be for those I interviewed and how deeply inspired I was by hearing their unique stories. Such work is a critical aspect of the quest to promote awareness of the importance of legacy. I strongly encourage us all to offer such opportunities to seniors in our communities.

Oral history has much value for us as elders and for our communities by preserving the stories of the people whose shoulders our lives are built upon. It enables us to learn from the experiences of those who have had the same aspirations and faced the same challenges as we do. This work is also a wonderful way for us to serve the elders in our communities, by offering them opportunities to review their lives in the presence of loving witnesses. If our questions are skillful, focusing on their strengths as they have dealt with life's difficulties, we can help them begin to reframe their experiences and create more empowering stories about their lives. In an age filled with technological wonders, there is no reason (other than lack of will or interest) that every older person cannot have an opportunity to tell their story and have it preserved. Imagine if every nursing home, assisted living facility, senior center, and faith community provided oral history opportunities for every client willing and mentally able to participate.

Conversely, having others do oral history work with us can be an important part of our own legacy work. It enables us to tell parts of our life stories in a way that enables those who view the recordings to hear our voices, see our expressions, and pick up all the nonverbal qualities that cannot be communicated in writing. Video-based oral history is a wonderful complement to (but not a replacement for) a legacy letter. There are nuances of thought and detail that require careful writing and rewriting, subtraction and addition, in order to be conveyed with the richness that can characterize such a letter. These generally are not possible in a video.

In doing oral history work with others or having others interview us, preparation is important. The interviewer and interviewee should spend time together a few days before the interview deciding the themes they will focus on. This gives the interviewee a chance to reflect and feel prepared and assures that she is emotionally invested in the process. I have often had prospective interviewees tell me that they are afraid they would be uncomfortable or inhibited by the camera. When this happens, I assure them that if they give it their best shot for five minutes and want to stop at that point, I will understand and honor their need. The reality is that I have never had anyone want to stop the process. In fact, many interviewees have felt frustrated when their session had to end because they felt as though they were just getting on a roll.

Once the interviewee feels ready to begin, I set up the camera, position the interviewee properly, lean forward, and begin a conversation, weaving in the questions as seamlessly as possible. It becomes a conversation between two people rather than an interview and is a comfortable, fulfilling experience for both of us.

Most of the people I know in their sixties and seventies have not asked anyone to do oral history work with them. Their thinking is that they may do this someday when they are really old and nearing their end, yet the reality is that we seldom know when our end is near or when we may lose our mental faculties. If you are serious about conscious eldering, it is important for you to do the work of focusing on your legacy now as a gift to those who follow you and because it is an integral part of your conscious preparation for elderhood.

In addition to recording the legacy you have already created, now is the time to start looking toward the future and the legacy you have yet to build. If our elderhood is to indeed be a time of fruition, the ripening of our emotional and spiritual growth, and an opportunity to use who we have grown into in service to the world around us, then the self that emerges from the passage out of midlife adulthood has a lot of legacy still to create. As we enter conscious elderhood, we honor the foundation of legacy built during our first several

decades of life. Upon this structure, a magnificent legacy of elderhood can be constructed in the chapters ahead. This legacy might
not be magnificent in the sense of being recognized and honored by
an unconscious world, but even so, it can be magnificent in the sense
that it is a shining beacon of consciousness, wholeness, service, and
love in a world urgently in need of light. Conscious elders work to
create such a legacy. A powerful tool for helping them achieve this is
one we call Ten Intentions for Ten Years.

Ten Intentions for Ten Years is a process designed to help you
bring the power of intention to the next segment of your life. This
process is most effective when you have already done significant
work in healing and letting go of your past, have spent time in the
neutral zone opening yourself to a vision for your elderhood, and
now feel the seeds of new beginnings emerging. On our Choosing Conscious Elderhood retreats, we introduce this practice after
participants have returned from their neutral zone time in nature.
If this practice is to be more than a conceptual exercise or an ego-
driven bucket list, it needs to be sourced by connection with your
inner guidance and the energy of your passion. It is for that reason
that I recommend that you do this as a practice of your reincorporation time when you sense new beginnings emerging. It is a practice
that involves reflection on the various aspects of your multidimensional life as an elder-in-the-making; your relationships; your inner
life; your use of your wisdom, skills, and gifts; what brings you joy;
what challenges enliven you; and your service to the community of
humans and of earth.

When you feel ready to engage in the Ten for Ten process, you
will begin to turn your inner promptings for action into written
intentions. It is useful to set a timeline for their completion (perhaps
ten years, perhaps five). What's important is that these intentions

become not merely fantasies but goals you are committed to achieving in whatever timeline you set. Recognize that these goals may shift as time passes, and you should be prepared to change course as your sense of guidance and your experiences suggest. But no matter how your goals may change over time, it is important that you bring the immense power of intention to all aspects of your life as you age.

As you begin putting your intentions into words, carefully choose the language you use. It is not empowering to write, "I hope that," or "I'd like to." That is only empty wishful thinking. It *is* empowering to declare, "Within ten (or five or however many) years, I will have," or "I intend to." As you write, it is likely that you will not immediately see the path toward accomplishing some of your goals. You may not have a road map or blueprint, but your intention sets a process in motion whereby the necessary steps reveal themselves, step by step. Your task is to trust the process and your sense of guidance, even in the face of adversity and uncertainty.

It is important when approaching your future with such intentionality that you do your best to have your intentions be more than just inspired words. *Envision* each of them being accomplished. *Feel* what you imagine you will feel when they are accomplished. *Write affirmations* that support achieving these goals. Once you have completed your list, use calligraphy, artwork, or some other means to visually express its significance to you and the depth of your commitment. When it is complete, place it on your home altar or in some other place where you will see it regularly. Reaffirm your commitments often and ask for spiritual support. It is also important to share your intentions with others who support your growth toward conscious elderhood. There is power in having others witness your intentions and in being able to ask for their support when acting on your intentions is difficult.

A couple of years ago I created my own Ten for Ten as a culmination of a long process of becoming aware of my needs in various spheres of my life in the years ahead. Below, I share several of my own intentions as an example of what such a list might encompass.

Within ten years, I *will* have

- Replaced my disempowering fears with deep trust in the Great Mystery that knows what I truly need to grow, serve, and thrive
- A strong, joyous relationship with my children, Mark and Brooke, and my grandchildren
- Helped my beloved wife, Barbara, fulfill her dream of earning her doctorate, and reveled with her in her accomplishment
- Fully developed my abilities as a writer and made a significant contribution to this world through books and articles
- Set aside at least one month each year for retreat—for deep spiritual practice
- Traveled with Barbara to Europe and other parts of the world
- Founded or helped create true community in which Barbara and I and others can grow, play, and learn
- Developed vibrant health through my lifestyle and through clearing out energy blocks in me that cause dis-ease
- Helped grow the Center for Conscious Eldering into a collective of colleagues who are a significant catalyst for promoting conscious eldering as the dominant paradigm for aging in contemporary society
- Found plenty of opportunities to fly-fish in beautiful places; continually increased my skill with rod, reel, and fly; and lovingly caught and released many trout
- Become a living model for others feeling called to conscious elderhood

At this point in my life, these intentions are important elements of my vision of what my life as a conscious, whole, contributing elder will be like. I trust that my vision will grow and evolve as I grow and evolve. As I grow in wholeness and make this evolving vision a reality, I am creating the next part of my legacy. I trust that when I leave this life, the legacy of my elder years will be one of service, of using my gifts as fully as possible, bringing love and compassion to everyone touched by my life, and being a peaceful, joyous being who shined a bright light in a dark world. Creating this legacy will be the greatest gift I can give to the generations that follow.

STORY BY THE FIRE
The Four Treasures That Have Informed My Life
by Reed Anderson

The legacy letter concept was first presented to me during a retreat at Ghost Ranch. What an extraordinary gift to be able to anticipate the moment of my death and have time to communicate thoughtfully with loved ones! About a year earlier, I had undergone surgery for an aggressive prostate cancer, and the notion of my own mortality had become quite vivid, to say the least. Momentarily putting these realities aside and taking on the task of writing a legacy letter to loved ones turned out to be just what I needed.

However, writing the letter wasn't a simple matter. First I had to convince myself that I had something of value to pass on. Then I had to focus my thoughts and feelings in a way that was entirely new to me. Given this opportunity, what would I write, and to whom? Did I want to say things that were specifically directed to my family and friends, or did I want my focus to be broader? Would I write about myself or about matters that seemed more universal?

I eventually decided that I would address my wife, my children, and my grandchild, as well as my friends from the Ghost Ranch retreat, my tai chi students, and the members of our local Buddhist sangha in Ramah, New Mexico. Once I had my audience in mind, I had to search my heart and bring into focus the values and aspirations I wanted to convey.

What I finally decided to write came from the work that Buddhism and many other spiritual paths encourage. I focused on the values that had been challenging for me to sustain in my own life and why, despite the struggle, they are worth cultivating. In my letter I wrote,

"Love, kindness, compassion, and forgiveness are four dispositions of the soul, four treasures that are worth any effort to cultivate in your life. They are the counterweights to other dispositions that need no cultivation at all because they arise from the ego, and the ego, unless educated away from its own nature, will always act in its own self-interest. Love, kindness, compassion, and forgiveness flow in the opposite direction. I can say at this point that whenever I can recall the experience of pain or strife in my life, there was an absence of one or more of these dispositions of the soul. I recall times when I had been unable to forgive, expecting compassion and love from others when it was I who should have been demonstrating these feelings toward them."

I tried to explain that it had taken a long time for me to affirm the centrality of these values in my life, and as I wrote, I had to question why this was the case. It was relatively easy to acknowledge the universal truth of these values, but it was a long time before I could overcome the notion that they were weak and impractical as guiding practices. In writing the legacy letter, I had to acknowledge that the process of making such values a real part of my everyday life would always be a challenge and a struggle, a path rather than an attainable goal.

For me, writing the legacy letter brought home the importance (and difficulty) of thinking deeply about my own values and aspirations. It also made me consider the difference I could make in the lives of my loved ones by sharing these things. My hope is that those who read my legacy letter will benefit from reading my words. It was with this in mind that I concluded my letter by saying that love holds the hand of kindness and compassion holds the hand of forgiveness. Together they have the power to change us and the world that is ours.

12

PRACTICES FOR BECOMING AND STAYING CONSCIOUS

I f we are to use significant life transitions to grow toward fulfilling our potential, then our passage from one life stage to another is not an easy one. It is indeed the journey of a hero. It is difficult to sever ourselves from an old sense of identity that is too constricting for the potential that wants to emerge in us. Then as we wait, wander, and wonder in the liminal limbo of the neutral zone, we often feel alone and lost, with little if any support. This is, of necessity, a time of fighting inner dragons in order to come to know and access our previously untapped strengths and potentials. Then gradually—often when all hope seems lost—rays of inner sunlight begin to illuminate our dark inner landscape. We feel blessed with increasingly frequent periods of clarity about our path forward into the new beginnings that call to us. Especially after the darkness of the neutral zone, our newly emerging vision, hope, and passion are precious gifts we want to hold on to. We have worked so hard to make it through this passage, and now we want with all our hearts to fully embrace our new beginnings. We want our vision of who we can be as conscious elders to remain strong and clear. We want to continue to feel confident and passionate. We have likely had profound moments of feeling connected to what is most authentic and essential in us, and we urgently want these experiences to continue. We've paid our dues. Now it's time to enjoy the rewards.

If only it were this easy. But it's not. These moments of illumination are your soul's precious gift to you, showing you what is possible. They come at those times when, for whatever reason, your soul is able to shine through those layers of personality that usually cover it and you see who you are truly capable of becoming. Our work as conscious elders-in-the-making is the work of embodying this powerful yet delicate vision of what can emerge in and through us. As anyone who has been deeply impacted by a vision quest, meditation retreat, spiritual practice, or unpredictable moment of grace knows, the work of integrating and embodying such transcendent experiences is the hardest work of all. This is the work that separates those seeking to get a temporary high from those committed to continual growth. Such moments of clarity and connection to our souls are ephemeral and easily obscured by the concerns of daily life, by our many light-blocking unconscious ways of thinking and behaving, and by all the unrecognized and untransformed aspects of ourselves. Much of the work of conscious eldering involves finding ways to bring more and more consciousness to our lives, because conscious awareness is what enables us to make choices that heal, transform, and enliven us.

However, even as we strive to live consciously, the periods of darkness between the flashes of light can be disheartening. I honor

Patricia Sun, a wise, compassionate, visionary teacher who lives in Berkeley, California, as the person who has contributed the most to my understanding of the workings of psyche and spirit. Many years ago she offered me what I consider the most important piece of wisdom about human growth I have ever received. I was struggling with periodic depression, darkness, and re-emergence of old emotional issues. These issues usually appeared a few days after I attended retreats or workshops that catalyzed moments of profound clarity and peace in me. "Why?" I asked. "What is wrong with me that I can't hold on to the state of heightened consciousness I know is possible?"

Patricia responded by essentially telling me that the journey of transformation is a process of becoming conscious of, and then transforming through love, the shadow parts of ourselves that do not fit our ideal for ourselves and that block our inner light from shining through. When we have experiences where our hearts open and our consciousness is raised, our ability to shine the light of consciousness on those dark areas within us is strengthened. Since we have this additional capacity, it is the nature of the growth process that shadow elements in us will rise to the surface so that we may become more conscious of them and work to transform them. Depression, a sense of inadequacy, and the rising of old issues after peak experiences are not an indication that we are inadequate but an affirmation that we are growing and are better equipped than before to do the inner work that supports our growth. Our challenge when we feel we have descended into a dark cave after reveling in the bright light at the mountaintop is to remember and trust the sincerity of our intention and the work our soul is doing to gradually but surely transform us. When old issues arise, our task is to do our best to send love to ourselves and our untransformed parts. This love is love that, while on the mountaintop, we knew was our essence and our destiny.

Don't let this reality discourage you. As you seek to grow into a conscious elder, you must become ever more aware of both your darkness (so that you can transform it) and your light (so that the best of you can shine through). This inner work, which requires commitment and effort, is what conscious eldering is all about.

Which Self Will Win

You may be familiar with the oft-told teaching story attributed to the Cherokee people in which the young person asks the wise elder, "Which wolf will win?" I'd like to offer you a revised version of this story as it relates to conscious eldering.

A passionate woman in her early sixties, feeling she was finally emerging from a difficult passage that had led her out of her midlife adulthood, approached a wise, wrinkled, white-haired elder widely recognized in the community as an exemplar of wisdom. The young emerging elder said to the wise elder, "I have within me a beautiful vision, or at least parts of a vision, of becoming like you. I have an inspiring sense of how I can use my best qualities, skills, and gifts to serve our community and be personally fulfilled as I age. I'm having some wonderful experiences of spiritual connection. My creativity seems to be coming to life again. I'm feeling more peace, joy, and optimism than I have in a long time.

"However, I'm also very aware of a whole other side to me. I often feel fear. Sometimes it is fear that I'm just deluding myself about conscious elderhood and that growing old is really just a drag. Sometimes it's fear that no matter what visions I have, there's no way I can achieve them in the real world I live in. Sometimes it's just a free-floating fear of the world and my life and the future. I'm also aware that I have so many habits that I can't seem to change that seem to numb me out.

My passion and optimism seem to fade so easily, and I don't know why. My heart feels open one day and closed the next. It seems there are two selves within me at war with each other. You're a wise elder. Please tell me: Which one will win?"

The elder looked into her eyes with compassion and responded, "The one you feed."

Toward the end of our Choosing Conscious Elderhood retreats, when participants have returned from their time of solitude doing neutral zone work, we focus on new beginnings. We discuss how to remain conscious when leaving the rarified air of a retreat setting. When we ask the group what they have learned about this from past experience, most sharing centers around adding new practices to their lives, such as meditation and journaling that support keeping the heart and mind open. Such practices are vitally important and can be effective; I will suggest some later in this chapter. However, at least as important are the things we choose to remove from our lives. Which self will win—whether we are increasingly able to live consciously or not—depends very much upon what self in us we feed. Healthy, conscious bodies, minds, and spirits cannot thrive on a physical, mental, and emotional junk food diet.

So I pose these questions for your reflection:

- Do you feed your body healthful, vitalizing foods most of the time?
- Do you feed your mind uplifting food such as poetry, beautiful music, artwork, inspiring films, and stories of people who help heal the world?
- Do you do your best to spend time with people who uplift you, support you, bring out the best in you, and don't drain you?
- Do you spend time amid the healing, soul-invoking energies of the natural world?

- Do you feed your spirit with activities and practices that bring you alive and make your heart sing?
- Do you feed yourself with the gift of doing your best to live consciously and intentionally?

We all feed ourselves plenty of devitalizing, disempowering, fear-inducing thoughts, media images, and experiences. Most of us have little awareness of the impact this has on us. It is extremely difficult to experience vision, inspiration, and passion for life when we are filling ourselves with toxins, no matter what spiritual practices we add to our lives. Conscious eldering implies a commitment to doing our very best to increase our awareness of what nurtures the best in us and what doesn't, and making lifestyle decisions that reflect this awareness. A conscious elder is committed to living more and more with intention and less and less out of habit.

Vision: Use It or Lose It

As I have discussed throughout this book, few people receive a full-blown vision of their unique calling and potential as an elder, along with a strategic plan for how to get there. We grow through the process of gradually unfolding this vision and using our creativity to achieve it, one step at a time. As incomplete as it may be, our intuition of what is possible may seem daunting. How can I ever accomplish this, especially when I see so little societal support for doing so? How can I ever reach that goal on the horizon when I can barely see how to get through the obstacles to a landmark fifty feet away?

The gift of vision is a double-edged sword; it can motivate us or harm us. One of the most important teachings in the rite of passage tradition is that when the energy of vision is not acted upon, it turns toxic. It wants expression, no matter how elementary or undeveloped. It's not just that it can fade if we don't somehow act on it, although this may well happen. It can also damage our psyche and even our body, turning into depression and lack of self-esteem. One of the most important ways we support staying conscious on our journey toward elderhood is to find ways to act on our sense of calling, even when we can't see the end goal or the route to it. This requires a deep commitment to trust in ourselves and our soul's guidance as we face fear. Fear of the unknown will not ever fully go away for most of us. However, the more we cultivate trust—the same trust that enabled us to let go of an identity that no longer fit, the same trust that guided us through the neutral zone to a place of new beginnings—the less impact fear will have on us. We trust that if we take the step immediately in front of us, the next one will become apparent. The path toward our sensed-but-not-seen goal may be a relatively straight line, or it may be much less direct, with unanticipated twists, turns, and backtracks. Either way, if we trust that inner guidance we have been courting throughout our journey of conscious eldering, we will continually grow in consciousness, fulfillment, and ability to serve and move ever closer to the goal on our horizon.

As you strive to reach your goal, I encourage you to find and commit to a practice that requires you to be conscious and awake. You are probably aware of a great diversity of spiritual practices and have engaged one or many of these. These can all be useful in our conscious eldering; the key is finding the practice(s) you truly resonate with, not just conceptually but experientially. We are each unique beings, and part of aging consciously is becoming aware of what truly makes a difference in our lives, as opposed to what we are told will make a difference. Sitting meditation may make a real difference for you, whereas a movement-based practice like qigong or hiking in nature may be what promotes growth in me. Working with paint and brush may open your creativity and intuition, while daily journaling will be what I most need to gain clearer access to my inner life.

The practice itself can be immensely important, but even more important is the commitment to practice, whatever the form. This commitment requires you to become conscious of your resistance to your growth and of the ways you have structured your life that support your status quo rather than growth. Commitment to a practice focuses you, awakens you from your many unconscious moments, and strengthens your ability to live with intention rather than habit.

The practices suggested in chapter 9 for opening yourself to vision, clarity, and spiritual connection while in the neutral zone also have much value in helping you be conscious of the guidance of your soul as you seek to grow the seeds of your new beginnings into the fruits of your elderhood. The new life stage you are entering is uncharted territory. You emerge into elderhood without a road map in a largely unconscious world that doesn't know, acknowledge, or honor what you feel called to become. Your dreams can offer clues to how to proceed. Synchronicities offer other clues and give you the awe-inspiring welcome experience that supports your journey and connects it to something larger than yourself. Solitude and silence remove you from the noise that keeps you from hearing that still, small voice within. Creative expression, in whatever form best fits you, gets your inner juices flowing and opens channels to the life energy in you that seeks outward expression. When you are truly alive, you embody creativity. Conscious elderhood is your soul's creativity expressed through your unique self. Strengthening your spiritual connection empowers everything else you do and helps assure that all your choices and actions are guided by your soul. Spending time in the natural world helps open you to what is most natural and authentic in yourself as you seek to create a map for your elderhood that supports your unique journey into and through a *conscious* elderhood.

Our efforts to aim high in our elderhood by feeding the best in ourselves and incorporating into our lives growth-supporting practices are critical. However, our best intentions may be incapable of countering the disempowering forces all around us if we do not have support. For this reason, conscious eldering is a journey that, for most of us, requires the support of others committed to the same goal. We will explore the need for community more fully in the next chapter.

STORY BY THE FIRE
Creating Spaciousness in My Elderhood
by Fran Weinbaum

Over the past year I have begun to use the word *spaciousness* to describe how I feel. I cannot recall that there was a particular incident or point at which this spaciousness began to appear, but I do know it was and continues to be a mind-body-soul type of experience. I experience it as a long exhale (again, on all levels) followed by a stillness and silence centered in my belly. There is both a sense of what is most important and precious and an ability to let it all go. There is a calmness and a poignant ability to act—strongly if necessary. There is patience and immediacy. Time is not important and time is now. The list of what I want to do is long, and yet I move slowly, deliberately, and spaciously through each day, knowing that there will be things left undone. I want space for emotions, for reflecting on and holding opposites, for silence, and for touching that place within that is both deep silence and deep love. At the end of each day I want to be able to say that I acted and spoke from my heart and did not use more than my share or, perhaps more truthfully, gave away more than I received.

All this came into clearer focus for me recently when I applied for a part-time job that was perfect for my experience and skills. The employer was a neighborhood association, and if I was hired, I would be responsible for leadership development within the resident community and on the board. The job also included promoting affordable housing and supervising the person hired to develop resident involvement. I sent in my application early, got an interview date, and did some background work. As my interest grew, so did my awareness of the dissonance with my chosen lifestyle. I continued to hold open the possibility, deciding that the interview would be an opportunity for me to ask questions of them and myself.

The first interview date was cancelled due to a couple of board members being ill. A week later, I made the one-hour drive to the interview only to discover that I had shown up on the wrong date. I felt pretty stupid for a moment and then, sitting in my car in the empty parking lot in front of the dark community building, I settled into considering the dissonance. This job was an hour from home, in a community that was not mine, and it would demand my attention way beyond the twenty hours a week in the job description. Plus, there were other wonderful opportunities to consider: work with a faith community in West Virginia to develop rites of passage for girls; a trip to the Czech Republic to coguide a women's rite of passage; a trip with my husband, Peter, to Scandinavia; and goat kids due at the end of March. What was I thinking?!

Driving home that day, I knew that I would withdraw from the hiring process. I would open up the space for the other things to happen without the pressure of competing priorities, or at least not more than already existed.

I went out to take care of the goats this morning, as usual. A bit distracted by already forgotten dreams from the night before and the things that needed to get done by noon, I did not immediately stop to say good morning to the land and sky. Walking toward the barn, I stopped with a gasp. The eastern sky was ablaze with deep pink and gray-blue clouds. Red sky in morning, sailors (and farmers) take warning. What a beautiful way to get the weather report. Smiling, I walked to the barn knowing I had made the right decision. Living with the spaciousness to see the morning sky year round is my choice.

I am exploring the possibilities for me to best contribute my gifts and asking myself whether I have the courage to stand on the front lines for the changes I believe need to happen. But as I make these choices, I am committed to creating an elderhood where my actions arise from the spaciousness I know I need to thrive.

13

FINDING SUPPORT
IN COMMUNITY

C ommunity is a critically important element of growing into conscious elderhood and enjoying this new chapter in your life. Research in neuropsychology has been validating what many of us see as obvious—that humans are social beings, wired to resonate with the beliefs and actions of those around us. This reality has survival value for our species, as it helps assure at least some level of the harmony societies need. It also makes significant cultural change very difficult, as the power of the entrenched beliefs and attitudes of the majority creates strong internal resistance to seeing any value in new ideas. As individuals committed to being conscious, we may see new possibilities for our lives and for the society we live in. However, being so strongly attuned to the values of those around us, for most of us, remaining conscious is nearly impossible if we try to do so in isolation. This is why it is important to find or create community with others who share our emerging vision and values while doing our best to lessen the influence of people and institutions whose values disempower our vision and commitment. Conscious eldering is a big, significant cultural paradigm shift. I know few (if any) people who have made much progress on this path in isolation. The support of community is necessary if conscious eldering is to become a way of living and growing and not merely an intriguing concept that makes little difference in the values we carry and the choices we make about how we age. Community empowers us; isolation weakens us. There is great power in individuals working together to discover and live their most cherished values. As Margaret Mead reminded us, "There is no doubt that a small group of committed citizens can change the world. Indeed, it is the only thing that ever has."

Some of us are fortunate to live in areas where people are exploring conscious eldering together. Many of us are not so fortunate, although I can assure you that this vision for aging is in the cultural wind, with people all over the world beginning to become aware of it or feeling discontent with the current disempowering models for aging. Creating or finding community to support you and others need not be daunting, but it does require some work and commitment.

One option for community is a conscious aging or conscious eldering discussion group in which participants meet regularly to share thoughts about aging, fears, hopes, challenges, and resources. Such groups are forming and meeting across North America in a variety of formats, some structured and some open-ended. If you can't find a group in your area, I encourage you to start one. Get the word out through your networks, place of worship, newspaper, or radio public service announcements. Sage-ing® International, the pioneering conscious aging organization, promotes effective discussion groups called the Wisdom Circle and makes available a free handbook on how to organize, recruit for, and conduct a Wisdom Circle. This organization also has members around North America who organize Wisdom Circles, workshops, and elder service projects in their states and provinces. (See the Resources section of this book for more information about Sage-ing International.) While the sense of personal connection and energy exchange that comes from meeting in person is preferable, there are an increasing number of groups that meet through telephone conference calls or via the internet. The format doesn't matter nearly as much as the commitment and creativity the organizers and participants bring to these supportive gatherings.

Another possibility is to find one or more friends who share your commitment and agree to work together on conscious eldering practices. Perhaps you can do structured life review work together and share your insights. You can write your legacy letters and share them with each other. Perhaps you can support each other in doing neutral zone work such as exploring dreams, supporting each others' creative expression, or spending periods of time in nature focusing on what needs to be let go as you age and your intimations of what possibilities lie ahead. You can share your intentions for the years ahead and offer each other encouragement for acting on these intentions. Your group may decide to read and discuss this book and then sequentially do the work suggested in these chapters so that you serve as guides to each other, moving through your extended rite of passage. Whatever you choose to do, it is so valuable to be able to share the process and results of your inner work with others. An additional value is that, by agreement, you can hold each other accountable for doing the inner work, offering encouragement, advice, or nudges as needed.

Yet another possibility is to find a life coach or counselor who understands your aspirations toward conscious elderhood and is supportive of them. Ask this person to witness and support your inner work, lend professional skill and perspective when needed, and help you hold yourself accountable for doing what you say you will do. There are many times when this inner work is not easy—no hero's journey is. These times are when the support of professionals can make a big difference in overcoming resistances that are deeply rooted in long-term inner dynamics and wounds.

As we enter the stage of new beginnings and gain a sense of calling to certain expressions of our elder gifts, it is essential that we act on this vision, however inchoate it may be at the time. It may well be a case of "use it or lose it." Having a supportive community can be especially critical at this time. When we feel called to do something out of the mainstream and cannot see the way forward—beyond a few possible steps, if that—obstacles may be everywhere, and the challenge of trying to move ahead with our vision may seem like too much for many of us. Having one or more friends to brainstorm with—perhaps help open doors for us, encourage us when we are down, and revel with us when we enjoy incremental successes—can make all the difference in the world.

Creating or participating in local service projects is another way for conscious elders to contribute to and benefit from community. It can be a very rewarding and supportive experience to join together to work on such projects while exploring what conscious aging is like for each of you and how you can bring more consciousness to your doing. A good model for such endeavors is the new Sages in Service project being created across North America by Sage-ing International. Many retired people offer their volunteer services in their communities these days. In fact, my community of Durango,

Colorado, is reputed to have more nonprofits per capita than any city in the United States. The vitality of many of these nonprofit organizations depends on the volunteer efforts of the many elders who have chosen to make Durango their home. It is possible to take this volunteer service even further by creating small groups that explore and support conscious eldering while serving the larger community with elder gifts and wisdom. The more consciousness we bring to our service, the more effective it will be and the more able we are to model elder wisdom and spirit in action.

While this book's focus is the inner work of conscious eldering, it is important that I share some of the significant changes happening at the macro level related to community that can have a great impact on the conscious eldering work of many people. Over the past fifteen to twenty years, an approach that is often called Aging in Community has created an ever-expanding menu of options for living environments for people as they age. Those who are pioneering these options see a great need for a third housing alternative for the vast generation of baby boomers now entering their elder years. Few people want to live in nursing homes or assisted living facilities as they experience losses of physical or mental abilities. The only mainstream alternative is to "age in place," living independently for as long as possible in one's home and relying on family or professional caregivers as abilities decline. When contrasted with the loss of dignity and independence that characterizes most facilities for the aged, aging in place certainly seems highly preferable. However, for a great many people, aging in place results in social isolation, loneliness, lack of stimulation, and absence of purpose. Rugged individualism at this point in life can result in lack of the community support and involvement that sustains both body and spirit.

Cohousing

The Aging in Community movement offers options for elders to maintain their sense of independence while having the support of community. One option is cohousing, whether intergenerational or devoted to elders only. In a cohousing community, homes are built around a central square, with the community having a kitchen and dining room for shared meals, a community meeting and recreation room, exercise facilities, rooms for creative projects, and other facilities designed to bring residents together. Individuals or couples own or rent their own homes, and they agree to be involved in setting policies for the community and to actively contribute to a mutually supportive community environment. Such a community structure encourages neighbors to help neighbors, using their talents in ways that bring them fulfillment while serving others. In some cohousing communities, residents who are interested join together to create service projects that benefit the larger community around them.

Villages

Growing even more rapidly is the village model, pioneered by the Beacon Hill Village in Boston, which was founded in 2002 and now has four hundred members. By the end of 2014 it is estimated that there will be more than two hundred villages spread across the United States, most with 150–300 members. In this model, people over fifty or sixty live in their own homes, usually in one section of a city, but enjoy many of the benefits of community. Villages are diverse groups of people representing a variety of backgrounds, talents, and interests. Members are encouraged but not required to take part in setting policies for the village. In fact, all they are required to do is pay a yearly fee, usually in the range of $500 or so, with reductions for those who cannot afford the full fee. This fee is used to hire village administrators who vet and contract with service providers such as home healthcare providers, home maintenance workers, plumbers, and tax preparers. These providers agree to provide their services to all members at a discounted rate. In addition, the administrators coordinate a village talent bank, through which members offer their talents to other village members and in return benefit from the talents of other members. For example, a village member needing transportation to the bank or doctor's office can count on another member to provide it. A member wanting life coaching may be able to count on having someone who can offer advice or a skilled listening ear when needed. As part of the village structure, opportunities are available for activities such as walking groups, tai chi classes, creative projects, and service projects in the community. Anyone who has something to share can announce their willingness and talents and easily make others aware of them and, hopefully, interested.

Communities of Shared Passions

Yet another creative option for aging in community is one that is still small in scope but has tremendous value for those who are attracted to it. This is a community living situation such as the Burbank Senior Artists Colony (BSAC) in California. In such communities, people over sixty who share a common passion live together in a large apartment building, condominium complex, or other arrangement, sharing communal facilities while engaging in the work they love. At BSAC, the residents share a theater, art studios, performance spaces, and other amenities that spark and support creative expression of all .

kinds. They have the opportunity to pursue their passions for as long as they are physically and mentally able, inspired and supported by kindred spirits.

These are three examples of the possibilities for enjoying and thriving in community as we age. While the residents in these types of communities will be widely diverse, it is inevitable that some of them will be called to conscious eldering. Those who are will find that they are perfectly placed to find mutual support for their growth within a larger community structure designed to support elders in whatever vision of aging they embrace.

The Sharing Solution

The Sharing Solution is a book by attorneys Janelle Orsi and Emily Doskow as well as a growing movement. It encourages the sharing with our neighbors of goods, services, space, wisdom, skills, and most anything else we can think of.[1] The benefits of sharing with others who live near us are many and obvious. Those who share save money, use less, and live more sustainably. Less obvious but perhaps more important is that sharing builds creative community, helping people of all ages break through the isolation of independent living.

Remembering the Community of Our Younger Days

As we review our lives, so many of us in the baby boom generation see that the moments we most cherish—the times we felt most alive—were times when we had the most community in our lives. For many, this community was found in college dormitories, or living hand-to-mouth with roommates in apartments or "student-quality" houses, or having wide circles of friends through our work, interests, or avocations. As we age, community diminishes for most of us. I don't believe this has to be so, and a great many other baby boomers—the generation that has led so many aspects of cultural change—agree. The idealism and passion so many of us experienced in our younger days remains alive in us, seeking to be awakened, and the emerging new vision for aging in all its manifestations and rainbow colors reflects this. Recognition of the importance of community is central to this new vision. Bolton Anthony, the visionary founder of the conscious aging organization Second Journey, eloquently expressed the importance of community in life's elder chapters when he wrote in *Aging In Community*, "We long for companions who will share our excitement for this 'second journey' in life—companions who will help sustain our own efforts to live more simply and authentically. For the paradoxical truth is, we never get to the bottom of ourselves on our own. Indeed, we only discover who we are face-to-face with others in work, love, and learning."[2]

If you truly feel called to conscious eldering, or at least to being more intentional about how you age, the role of community in your life needs to be addressed. To do so, I encourage you to reflect on these questions: Does anything in this chapter speak to you? Do you feel isolated from others who share your values and aspirations? Do you have a yearning for more community with people who share your values? If you desire more community, what internal and external challenges stand in the way of achieving this? Your answers to these questions can make a big difference in your growth, fulfillment, and quality of life in your elder years. Perhaps finding community does not feel like your path on the road ahead. Reflect carefully on this and make the choices that feel most authentic and supportive for you. But be aware that you have a choice in the matter. With a bit of courage, creativity, and willingness to step outside the cultural mold and your present comfort zone, you can grow in love, passion, and service in community with others. Together you can be one of those small groups of committed citizens changing the face of aging in the world.

STORY BY THE FIRE
The Power of Circles
by Anita McLeod

When I was in my midlife and going through menopause, I had experiences with doctors and other healthcare professionals that left me confused and frustrated. I did not believe I needed drugs or hormone replacement therapy (HRT) to be healthy, and I was concerned about the side effects. I told my doctor my concerns about HRT and that I would not be following his advice for now. His irritated, dismissive response left me determined to learn as much as I possibly could about healthy menopause.

I began by attending lectures by women physicians and reading medical literature, which was depressing. They put a disease spin on a normal life transition. All the words were about disintegration, deterioration, disease, and loss, while I was feeling vibrant, healthy, and strong. The mismatch between the medical model and my experience was glaring. I readjusted my search to books supporting a focus on creating health and wellness during menopause. The information in these few resources was enough to create a framework for a workshop series I developed and led at Duke University through the employee wellness department, where I had been leading health promotion programs for several years. Sixteen women gathered in a circle during

the lunch hour once a week for four weeks. As I listened to the participants speak of their experiences and discover their knowing, I often
felt chills run up one side of my body and down the other. What happened in this group led to the creation of many "healthy menopause"
circles over the next ten years.

What most struck me about these groups is that women usually
showed up the first time filled with fear. Woman after woman said
that her body felt out of control, as I had felt when I first made an
appointment with the doctor. As we told our stories, we discovered
that we were not alone, which greatly reduced our fear and stress. In
listening to ways others found to cope with their challenges, we found
creative ways to cope with our own. In the safety of the group, we
gradually spoke of our vulnerabilities, strengths, and yearnings. The
depth of sharing and compassion the women had for themselves and
each other gave us all courage to speak from deeper parts of ourselves,
connect our perceptions, and create meaning out of our suffering. We
began to define for ourselves the meaning of our midlife experience.

When I entered my sixties, I once again felt like I was walking into
unfamiliar territory without a map or guide. I signed up to participate in a conscious eldering rite of passage program and experienced
the powerful process of council—speaking from the heart, listening
with the ears of the heart, and being aware of the impact of our words
on the group. These guidelines, along with Christina Baldwin's circle
basics described in her book *Calling the Circle*, became the foundation for my future work as an elder. As I recalled my experience with
midlife groups, I decided to offer "women over sixty" circles to explore
the possibilities, challenges, and gifts of aging. To explore conscious
aging, we need both solitude and community to help us listen to our
deeper selves and discover our personal truths. We create a circle to
support the internal journey of each person, a circle that helps them

feel safe enough to develop a relationship with their inner wisdom. In the circle we also learn from each other. We practice presence.

As I move into my seventies, I continue to seek sacred circles where my soul will feel safe enough to speak out and I will have the gift of hearing others' souls speak—in places where elders may mirror and support each other, places where they can reflect and shine their light on the inner light of others, midwifing inner wisdom. In circle, in community, we find companions to journey with through our elder years. We help each other make meaning of our life experience and discover the wisdom we want to pass on to future generations. We support each other in taking meaningful action in the world.

CONCLUSION

As this book comes to an end, I ask you to recall Stan and Carol, whose contrasting life choices after retirement headed up this book's Introduction. Stan sees his retirement as the end of his years of growth and contribution, while Carol sees herself as an elder who is continually growing and serving. By examining the difference between their perspectives on their aging, we can identify the essence of conscious eldering and see how it offers a very different, empowering perspective on what aging can mean to individuals and to society.

Stan has made some lifestyle choices, including choosing a generally healthy diet and committing to regular exercise, that support his physical well-being and make it likely that he will be able to be active for many years after his retirement. He will probably be able to bike, play racquetball, and travel, enjoying activities that many in the generations before him would not have considered possible for someone past retirement age. I imagine that his wife, who is quite active in the community, will eventually motivate or persuade him to engage in more volunteer activities. He enjoys spending time with his grandchildren, who live nearby, although he says he has trouble relating to them. Stan has what a great many aging baby boomers consider a good life—one that is quite attractive to those in midlife who look forward to retirement. He appears to be satisfied with his life and enjoying being free of professional stressors and financial concerns. Advocates of Positive Aging might point to Stan as an example of someone who is aging well and living a more active and personally empowered life than many in his generation or preceding ones.

Outwardly, Carol's life is similar to Stan's. She enjoys travel and hobbies and being a patron of the arts. She makes lifestyle choices that support her health and vitality. She is fortunate to be free of financial concerns and full-time professional stressors. She is an active volunteer in her community and with a national organization, albeit much more than Stan at this point. Many would feel that Carol also has a good life. Here the similarities end.

Unlike Stan, Carol has a vision for her aging that upholds her continuing personal and spiritual growth as her highest values. She knows that this growth and the inner work that makes it possible is meeting an important need of her soul now and will be even more critical when later elderhood arrives and her ability to be physically and socially active wane. In the midst of her outward activity, she is focused on cultivating her relationship with her soul—with being—as the source of her ability to serve others now and as her truest identity as her abilities gradually wane. Carol sees herself as an elder—or perhaps more accurately as a woman ever-growing into her potential to use her gifts and wisdom as an elder in her community. She views her strong relationship with her grandchildren and her deep commitment to the organizations she is involved with as important opportunities for sharing her elder wisdom and gifts. Feeling strongly attuned to a sense of calling from deep within her, Carol is aiming high as she ages, wanting the elder chapters of her life to be the period when her rich legacy reaches its fruition.

The Positive Aging models serve many people well as they age. These models offer a certain sense of empowerment in a culture where any empowerment of its seniors is a welcome change. They help many people achieve a certain level of satisfaction and mental wellness without paying attention to growth in consciousness, wisdom, or ability to know and respond to the promptings of their souls. For many people, these models basically enable individuals to continue to bring their midlife selves into their senior years, prolonging midlife for as long as possible.

However, for those feeling a call to aim higher, Positive Aging is not enough. It does not deal with the whole person and stresses adaptation to aging rather than the transformation aging invites. Those feeling this call realize that preparing for the passage into true elderhood and ultimately into the Great Beyond requires a gradual shedding of identification with their ego selves in order to allow the light of their soul to shine through. They realize that this requires difficult, persevering inner work where the primary focus is on goals beyond personal satisfaction and enjoyment, although these may be part of the journey. They approach their lives feeling that "having something to do" with their days will not satisfy their inner needs as the elder within seeks expression. They know that the journey ahead will take courage and lots of heart and require their best efforts at a time when many people their age want to let go of making an effort.

Conscious eldering is not a path everyone will embrace. Aging is difficult, and I honor all those who are doing their best to age well in a confusing and not very conscious cultural milieu. Certainly, many people are not able to hear the inner call to elderhood amid the many other cultural voices and do the best they can with the awareness they have. Others feel discontented with the dominant vision for aging but have no awareness of what this feeling means or what alternatives are available. However, a growing number of baby boomers and those beyond their sixties are indeed hearing the call to age consciously. Are you one of them? What do you plan to do with the remaining chapters of your one precious life?

If this book has helped you recognize that call within yourself, I encourage you to respond to that call as if your inner life and deepest fulfillment depend upon it, as if the well-being of the generations to follow depends upon the choices people like you and me make now. I encourage you to begin that journey now, for you don't know how much time you will have to fulfill your potential. Begin now, because while your gifts may not seem significant, collectively our commitments and gifts can and will make a critical difference in helping us meet the huge challenges facing today's wounded world as we lay the foundation for a healthy world in which our descendents can thrive. There is no greater legacy that we can leave for the generations that will follow us and no greater gift that we can give ourselves than to aim high as we age, ever reaching for our best. The world needs the wholeness, wisdom, and gifts of conscious elders.

ACKNOWLEDGMENTS

No personal quality more strongly characterizes conscious elderhood than gratitude. Gratitude is both a powerful practice that opens the heart to the trust and healing essential to conscious eldering and a way of life, a state of being, that this inner work leads to. As I have gone through the process of writing this—my first book—gratitude has been more abidingly present for me than ever before. It has been a precious and unanticipated gift that has kept my confidence strong in those times of doubt about whether I really have anything meaningful to share. Throughout my writing, I have often recalled with deep gratitude all those whose experiences, wisdom, and support are reflected in these words, without whom this book and my own journey of conscious eldering would not have been possible.

I am grateful to Patricia Sun, whose beautiful soul touched mine, giving me the precious experience of knowing what wholeness feels like and setting me on my path toward growth into the wholeness I felt when with her. I am grateful to Barbara Courtney, who for nearly thirty-five years has offered deep insight into my soul's guidance, especially during dark times when I could see little light anywhere. My deep gratitude to my dear mentors Meredith Little and the late Steven Foster, founders of the School of Lost Borders, who taught me the power of rites of passage but even more importantly showed me what passionate, unwavering dedication to a calling looks like.

I honor Elizabeth and Robert Cogburn for teaching me the immense power of ceremony for transforming lives, for more than thirty years of friendship, and for modeling for me and many others what truly conscious elderhood can be. My gratitude to Cynthia Leav Bolender, my partner for many years in offering wilderness vision quests. You did much, Leav, to help me recognize the power of the feminine on my journey toward wholeness. For inviting me to the path of conscious eldering when they asked me thirteen years ago to join them in creating and presenting the first Choosing Conscious Elderhood vision quests and retreats, I will be ever grateful to Wes Burwell and Ann Roberts, two wise elders whose lives embody what they teach so effectively. Thank you to Elena Burton, a dear friend of many years whose soul resonates with mine in a way that words cannot describe. And to Jan Milburn for giving me life-changing experiences of the power of indigenous wisdom through our pilgrimages together to Copper Canyon.

The Sage-ing philosophy and practices of Rabbi Zalman Schachter-Shalomi have played an important role in shaping my understanding of the possibilities for aging consciously and the inner work that can help make this possible. I am deeply grateful to

Reb Zalman and the many leaders in Sage-ing® International, from whom I have learned much and whose support has been critical in the development of my work, which is strongly grounded in Sage-ing as well as in the wisdom of the rite of passage tradition. I especially acknowledge and thank Gary Carlson, a cofounder and key leader in Sage-ing International who gradually and skillfully drew me into this pioneering organization. When I'm with you, Gary, my creativity (and it seems yours also) in envisioning ways to share conscious aging come to life. And I honor Robert Atchley, who thinks of himself as an "ordinary Sage," but for so many committed to Sage-ing; he is an extraordinary model for the kind of elder we hope to grow into.

There are many, many others whose support, encouragement, and wisdom have been critical in creating opportunities for me to do my heart's work, deepen my understanding of conscious eldering, create the Center for Conscious Eldering, and grow to the point where I could write this book. While I can't name you all here, I especially thank Rick Medrick of Outdoor Leadership Training Seminars, who gave me my opportunity to start working with rites of passage; Bill Plotkin, whose Animas Valley Institute sponsored our early Choosing Conscious Elderhood programs and from whom I have learned much about soul-centered human development; Harry R. (Rick) Moody, networker extraordinaire, who continues to teach me the importance of creating synergy through collaboration with others who share a common vision; Fran Weinbaum and Rosemary Cox, whose writing and conversations with me provided valuable insight into the dynamics of forgiveness and grief; and Anne Wennhold, my primary partner these days in offering conscious eldering retreats. You show us younger elders how to move into later elderhood with grace, dignity, lightheartedness, and wisdom, Anne. Our work together has been one of the great privileges of my life.

To those intrepid, committed conscious elders-in-the-making whom I have been privileged to guide on retreats and workshops and who have contributed so very much to my understanding of what the path of conscious eldering is about: thank you for your honest sharing of your fears, challenges, and visions for your elderhood, and for the opportunity to do the work that is my calling. When I was creating my proposal for this book, many of you offered to contribute written stories from your personal experiences with conscious eldering. I knew that your stories would help bring to life for the readers the concepts I present, and I am deeply grateful to you. I received stories from more than thirty people and was able to include only the twelve stories written by Helene Aarons, Diane Allan, Reed Anderson, Cathy Carmody, Anette Edens, Joe H., Judith Helburn, Lucia Leck, Anita McLeod, Jonathan Parker, Susan Prince, and Fran Weinbaum. Those whose stories of courage and heart that did not make it into the book but did inspire me and inform my thinking include Linda Blachman, Robert Croonquist, Maureen Dobson, Maggie Dulany, Penny Dunning, Phyllis Eisner, Barbara Fairfield, Margo Frank, Mike Hughes, Robert King, Arden Mahlberg, Susan Manning, Roger Merchant, Jackie Merrill, Randy Morris, Margaret Sarkissian, Carol Scott-Kassner, Paul Severance, Anne Wennhold, and Carol Wilburn.

I never planned to write a book until I received that fateful phone call from editor Emily Han at Beyond Words Publishing asking me if I'd ever considered writing a book on conscious aging. Emily's continual encouragement helped me see that this book was not only possible and doable but also important. I am grateful to you, Emily, and your colleagues at Beyond Words for seeing and trusting my potential, and for helping me to do so as well. You opened one of the most important doors of my life. Once my manuscript was written, Sarah Heilman applied her editing magic to it, teaching me a lot about the difference between pretty good writing and a more effective, polished presentation. Thank you, Sarah. Your skills shine through this book.

Perhaps most important, I am filled with gratitude for my family. My father, Albert Pevny, introduced me to the natural world and showed me the healing power of standing in moving waters, ostensibly fishing for trout. I thank my children, Mark and Brooke, for your support and understanding over many years when people asked you what your dad did for a living and you did your best to explain something that certainly was not easy for you and others to understand. And finally, I offer my very strongest gratitude to Barbara Donica Pevny, my wife and life partner of forty years, without whose unwavering support little that I have accomplished would have been possible. When I had little faith in myself, you had mountains of faith in me. You have sacrificed much to allow me to follow my oftentimes ill-defined dream, and for your love and support I dedicate this book to you. I pledge my support as you pursue your personal dreams and we grow together into a love-filled conscious elderhood.

EXERCISES

Throughout this book I have presented a variety of practices, several of which I have gathered here for your convenience. I suggest that you work with these exercises in conjunction with reflection upon the chapters in which they are found. Keep in mind that these exercises and the other practices recommended throughout the book are most effective when used within the context of doing the inner work of the stages of transition this book presents.

The Practice: Life Review

Life review is the foundation for much of the inner work of conscious eldering. It is our opportunity to come to terms with where we have traveled to reach this point of departure into a new chapter. It is the way that we recall our often long-forgotten experiences and bring to awareness what we learned—or still have the opportunity to learn—from those events. As we age, there is a natural tendency to look back on our lives. Doing this in a focused way is a powerful practice. There are many ways to engage in life review. You may use all of them or just a few.

The Process

- Break your life into seven year segments. For each segment, reflect on and write about your strongest memories; the most influential people in your life; the most difficult or painful experiences; the most joyous or enlivening experiences; and how this life chapter may be impacting your life now. Some people like to integrate artistic expression into this process. An especially impactful way to do this is to imagine your life as encompassing the cycle of a year, with January being your first seven years; February, ages eight to fourteen; October, ages sixty-four to seventy and December, seventy-eight plus.
- Look at your life thematically. Reflect on and write about the important people in your life; the development and use of your talents; the evolution of your spiritual life; the wounds and losses you experienced; the biggest challenges and how you dealt with them; the people, things, and experiences that brought you the

most joy and made you feel most alive; and the values you have
come to hold most dear.

• Write an autobiography in which you tell the story of your
  life's most significant events and learnings to your children or
  descendants.

• Have a friend do oral history work with you, preferably using
  video to capture you telling you stories.

• Participate in life review workshops. Various individuals offer
  these in the United States and elsewhere.

You may also search "Life Review Resources" online to find a
variety of helpful tools. There is no limit to how many life review
processes you may utilize, and you may find that different processes
work for you at different times. However you choose to do your life
review work, what is most important is to recall key experiences and
reflect on what they mean for you now. Successful life review is about
calling up memories to gain insight into your new life.

The Practice: Writing a Legacy Letter

A legacy letter is a precious gift to our descendants. Its creation is an important gift to ourselves as well. It differs from a typical eulogy in that it's not just a recitation of your positive qualities. It differs from some definitions of an ethical will in that it is not just a listing of values you want to communicate. It is not merely a family history, although elements of that can be woven in. Rather, I recommend that you view this as an opportunity to paint a verbal picture for your descendants of who you were.

If you choose to write a legacy letter as part of your conscious eldering work, begin by doing your best to imagine that you have only a limited time to live—perhaps one month or six months. This gives a sense of poignancy and urgency to your writing. Then try to get a sense of who you are writing this letter for (besides yourself), as this can help move this process from the realm of abstraction to emotion-infused reality. You might write your legacy letter with a specific grandchild or grandchildren in mind or address it to some other child who is important in your life, or you might write to future descendants several generations removed. Once you feel your letter is complete, you can decide how and when to make it available to whomever it is addressed, knowing that you can add to it later or can create an addendum that reflects the legacy of your elderhood. It is often the case that young children or grandchildren will find it a precious gift further down the road.

Write about what you would most like them to know about your life: events and people that played the most significant roles in shaping who you became; your biggest challenges and weaknesses and how you dealt with them; key turning points; your most dearly held values; your spirituality; the personal qualities and skills that helped define you as the unique person you have been.

A legacy letter is not something to be done in one sitting; rather, it is an unfolding project that is best seen as a piece of your ongoing inner work to heal and honor your past as your unique expression of the universal hero's journey of growth.

The Practice: Letting Go of Your Past

In order to move forward, you must be willing to let go of parts of yourself and your life that keep you bound to your past. Many people find that employing a ceremony can help with this transition. You may want to use a ritual to support letting go of several aspects of your past, or you may wish to create a separate ceremony for each one when the time feels right. Although the emotions surrounding these ceremonies may be complex, the ceremony itself is fairly simple.

The Process

- Start by finding or creating some physical object that symbolizes an old skin to be shed. The selected object may be photos, letters, or any other object that you strongly associate with some aspect of your life that needs to be shed.
- Spend time with this object, investing it with the energy of what it represents. Before your ceremony, place it in a special place in your home, such as an altar, where it gathers your emotional and spiritual energy for a period of time.
- Build a fire to burn your object or dig a hole to bury it in. You may choose to do this part alone or with others present. Many find that having the support of others can be empowering and affirming.
- As you stand over the fire, speak about the significance of the part of your life you are letting go of as well as why it is important for you to let go now. Finish by stating, plainly and firmly, your intention to let go of this item and all that it symbolizes.
- Approach the fire, feeling love and commitment for your growth, and place the item in the flames.

The Practice: The Death Lodge

The Death Lodge is designed to help you remember the important events of your life and bring completion to important relationships. These events and relationships may look very different with your new awareness of your mortality than they did when they occurred, so reflecting on them now can give you great insight.

The Process

- Find a place of silence and solitude. Many people find that being in nature works best for them, but ultimately this should be a safe place where you feel comfortable.
- Before you enter, offer a prayer or state an intention that the Great Mystery, however you name it, be with you, supporting and guiding your work. You might bless and purify your Lodge with incense or bring in some flowers. Be sure to bring with you your journal and perhaps an object you consider sacred.
- Reflect on how you have used your gifts throughout your life, acknowledge your strengths and weaknesses, and forgive yourself for the harm you have done to others. Take the time to explore your relationship with the Great Mystery throughout your life and at this time of transition.
- When the time feels right, invite the spirits of those who have been important in your life to visit you, one at a time. These may be the spirits of people who are alive, with whom healing needs to happen, and with whom you could have a face-to-face conversation. You can use the Death Lodge to practice what you will say to each person and to make the commitment to try your best to meet with them in person.

- You can invite others who are alive but with whom a face-to-face meeting is impossible. Picture them in your Lodge with you. Imagine yourself talking to their spirits, saying what you need to say, and hearing what they say in response. You can have this conversation in your imagination or in your journal if writing helps make it tangible.

- You can invite people who have died and with whom you never had the opportunity to share what's in your heart. Again, speak to their spirits and imagine what those wise, loving spirits have to say to you. It's OK if you cannot connect with a sense of what their spirits have to say and only remember their hurtful selves. Speak the truth of your heart, doing your best to recognize and honor their role in your growth while acknowledging the pain they may have caused you.

- Forgive and honor yourself. For many people, this is the most important and difficult part of Death Lodge work, but nothing closes our hearts and fills us with conflict more than self-hatred. Here we have the opportunity to forgive these parts of ourselves for their weakness and to thank them for what they have taught us about our shadows and our most dear values. From a conscious perspective, we can dialog with and extend love to these parts of us with the goal of re-owning disowned aspects of ourselves. The more we do this, the more whole we become.

It is important to note that the Death Lodge practice is not something you do only once. Rather, it is an ongoing process that you can use to help heal yourself and your relationships. You can bring more wholeness to your elderhood and be ready for that final day, whenever it may come.

The Practice: Understanding and Using the Wisdom of Dreams

As noted in chapter 9, there is no hard and fast rule for interpreting dreams, but they can be a great source of insight and wisdom. To utilize this insight, it is important to somehow capture on paper or audio recorder enough of the dream so that you don't lose it as soon as you become active. Then when you are ready, you can attend to the dream.

The Process

- First, write the dream (or tell the dream to someone who really cares) in the present tense. This helps make the dream more immediate so that you are experiencing it again, rather than merely recounting it.

- Then write (or tell) the dream again, this time acknowledging every element in the dream as a part of yourself. It is understood that "you" in the dream is your everyday personality self. Here's an example: "I am in the desert (of myself) walking down a deep canyon (of myself). My walk is peaceful until I hear a rustle in the thick brush (of myself) and, when I turn to look, see a large mountain lion (of myself) only several yards away. At first I am terrified and want to run, but I remember that running is the most dangerous thing I could do. As I stand there in terror, with the lion (of myself) just looking at me, a white-haired elder woman (of myself) appears around a bend in this canyon (of myself). This elder woman (of myself) approaches me and tells me . . ."

- After this second writing or telling, reflect on what the key images in the dream represent to you. What associations do you have with the desert? What does desert represent in you? What in you might a mountain lion represent?
- You might also try to start a dialog with the key images from your dream. Using your journal, try addressing the lion. Ask why it has shown up on your hike. Tell it about your fear of it and allow it to respond to you. Address the elder woman. You may be surprised at how such dialogs begin to have life and feel real, providing insight not normally accessible to your rational mind.

If you find that your dream has provided guidance of some sort, look for a way to apply that guidance in your life in a tangible way as soon as possible. This can mean creating some simple ritual to acknowledge the guidance or setting an intention for some inner change or outer action.

The Practice: Ten Intentions for Ten Years

Ten Intentions for Ten Years is a process designed to help you bring the power of intention to the next segment of your life. This process is most effective when you have already done significant work in healing and letting go of your past, have spent time in the neutral zone opening yourself to a vision for your elderhood, and now feel the seeds of new beginnings emerging. On our Choosing Conscious Elderhood retreats, we introduce this practice after participants have returned from their neutral zone time in nature. When you feel ready to engage in the Ten for Ten process, you will begin to turn your inner promptings for action into written intentions.

The Process

- Start by setting a timeline for their completion—perhaps ten years, perhaps five. What's important is that these intentions become not merely fantasies but goals you are committed to achieving in whatever timeline you set. Recognize that these goals may shift as time passes, and you should be prepared to change course as your sense of guidance and your experiences suggest. But no matter how your goals may change over time, it is important that you bring the immense power of intention to all aspects of your life as you age.

- As you write out your ten intentions, use empowering language. It is not empowering to write, "I hope that," or "I'd like to." It *is* empowering to declare, "Within ten years, I will have," or "I intend to." As you write, it is likely that you will not immediately see the path toward accomplishing some of your goals. You may not have a road map or blueprint, but your intention sets a process in motion whereby the necessary steps reveal themselves, step by step. Your task is to trust the process and your sense of guidance, even in the face of adversity and uncertainty.

• It is important when approaching your future with such intention-ality that you do your best to have your intentions be more than just inspired words. *Envision* each of them being accomplished. *Feel* what you imagine you will feel when they become realities in your life. Write affirmations that support your achieving these goals. Once you have completed your list, use calligraphy, art-work, or some other means to visually reflect its significance to you and the depth of your commitment.

When your list is complete, place it on your home altar or in some other place where you will see it regularly. Reaffirm your com-mitments often and ask for spiritual support. It is also important to share your intentions with others who support your growth toward conscious elderhood. There is power in having others witness your intentions and in being able to ask for their support when acting on your intentions is difficult.

RECOMMENDED BOOKS FOR
AGING MORE CONSCIOUSLY

Aging as a Spiritual Practice: A Contemplative Guide to Growing Older and Wiser by Lewis Richmond (Gotham Books, 2012)

Aging in Community, edited by Janice M. Blanchard (Second Journey Publications, 2013)

The Big Shift: Navigating the New Stage Beyond Midlife by Marc Freedman (PublicAffairs, 2011)

Broken Open: How Difficult Times Can Help Us Grow by Elizabeth Lesser (Villard Books, 2004)

Calling the Circle: The First and Future Culture by Christina Baldwin (Random House, 2009)

Claiming Your Place At the Fire: Living the Second Half of Your Life on Purpose by Richard J. Leider and David Shapiro (Berrett-Koehler Publishers, 2004)

The Elder by Marc Cooper and James Selman (Sahalie Press, 2011)

Encore: Finding Work that Matters in the Second Half of Life by Marc Freedman (PublicAffairs, 2008)

Essential Spirituality: The 7 Central Practices to Awaken Heart and Mind by Roger Walsh (Wiley and Sons, 1999)

Ethical Wills: Putting Your Values on Paper by Barry K. Baines (Perseus Publishing, 2001)

Falling Upward: A Spirituality for the Two Halves of Life by Richard Rohr (Jossey-Bass, 2011)

The Final Crossing: Learning to Die in Order to Live by Scott Eberle (Lost Borders Press, 2006)

The Five Stages of the Soul: Charting the Spiritual Passages That Shape Our Lives by Harry R. Moody with David Carroll (Anchor Books, 1998)

The Force of Character: And the Lasting Life by James Hillman (Random House, 1999)

From Age-ing to Sage-ing: A Profound New Vision of Growing Older by Zalman Schachter-Shalomi and Ronald S. Miller (Grand Central Publishing, 2014)

Fruitful Aging: Finding the Gold In the Golden Years by Tom Pinkson (self-published, 2012)

I Will Not Die an Unlived Life: Reclaiming Purpose and Passion by Dawna Markova (Conari Press, 2000)

Live Smart After 50! The Expert's Guide to Life Planning for Uncertain Times by Life Planning Network (50 contributing writers) (Life Planning Network, 2012)

Nature and the Human Soul: Cultivating Wholeness and Community in a Fragmented World by Bill Plotkin (New World Library, 2008)

The Power of Purpose: Find Meaning, Live Longer, Better by Richard J. Leider (Berrett-Koehler Publishers, 2010)

Prime Time: How Baby Boomers Will Revolutionize Retirement and Transform America by Marc Freedman (PublicAffairs, 1999)

The Roaring of the Sacred River: The Wilderness Quest for Vision and Self-Healing by Steven Foster and Meredith Little (Prentice Hall Press, 1989)

Second Journeys: The Dance of Spirit in Later Life, edited by Bolton Anthony (Second Journey Press, 2013)

Soul Mission, Life Vision: Recognize Your True Gifts and Make Your Mark in the World by Alan Seale (Red Wheel/Weiser, 2003)

Still Here: Embracing Aging, Changing, and Dying by Ram Dass (Riverhead Books, 2000)

The Third Chapter: Passion, Risk, and Adventure in the 25 Years After 50 by Sara Lawrence-Lightfoot (Sarah Crichton Books, 2009)

Transitions: Making Sense of Life's Changes by William Bridges (Addison-Wesley, 1980)

True Purpose: 12 Strategies for Discovering the Difference You Are Meant to Make by Tim Kelley (Transcendent Solutions Press, 2009)

What Really Matters: 7 Lessons for Living from the Stories of the Dying by Karen M. Wyatt (Select Books, 2011)

What Should I Do with the Rest of My Life: True Stories of Finding Success, Passion, and New Meaning in the Second Half of Life by Bruce Frankel (Penguin, 2010)

Women's Lives, Women's Legacies: Passing Your Beliefs and Blessings to Future Generations by Rachael Freed (Fairview Press, 2003)

A Year to Live: How to Live This Year as If It Were Your Last by Stephen Levine (Bell Tower, 1997)

ORGANIZATIONS THAT SUPPORT AGING CONSCIOUSLY

The following organizations are members of the Conscious Aging Alliance. They represent a diversity of approaches to empowering older adults. Some of these approaches focus primarily on the outer lives of people in or approaching their elder years; others focus explicitly on conscious aging, helping older adults grow emotionally and spiritually. All these approaches are important, and I believe none alone is sufficient in helping develop conscious elders whose inner and outer lives reflect wholeness.

The Center for Conscious Eldering, based in Durango, Colorado, offers Choosing Conscious Elderhood Rite of Passage retreats, Coaching for Conscious Living, and Meeting Ancient Wisdom Pilgrimages for participants to meet indigenous elders. It serves those in and approaching the elder third of life who seek passion, purpose, growth, and service as they age. A unique and important aspect of the programs is incorporating the power of nature in support of personal growth as an elder; retreats, workshops, and pilgrimages all involve significant time spent outdoors in inspiring natural settings. www.centerforconsciouseldering.com

Fierce with Age: The Online Digest of Boomer Wisdom, Inspiration and Spirituality features daily and bi-weekly summaries and excerpts of the best web-based writing about spirituality and aging for boomers. In addition, Fierce with Age offers self-guided online retreats on the subject of spirituality and aging. www.fiercewithage.com

Gray Is Green encourages older Americans to respond to unprecedented ecological challenges. Actions may range from block-votes for policy changes to mass market demands for sustainable living choices in housing, food, transportation, healthcare, and urban design. Gray-Greens possess unique gifts for adaptive response; in witnessing the cumulative environmental legacy modern society is leaving to our children and grandchildren, they hear the call to action. Periodic email updates and news items for sustainable living and environmental advocacy as well as access to an archive of information resources are available by signing up on the website. www.grayisgreen.org.

The Institute of Noetic Sciences has developed a Conscious Aging Program for seniors who are ready to embrace the final stage of their journey as a prime opportunity for spiritual, emotional, and psychological growth. It consists of an eight-session workshop series designed to shift participants' consciousness from self-limitation, lack, isolation, and fear toward expansiveness, inclusiveness, wholeness, connection, and compassion. Session Plans can be combined and conducted as an eight-lesson series, as a smaller series of several sessions, or presented individually, as each session has been developed to stand alone as a complete program. This program includes a companion workbook for participants, which is also available to the general public. For more information, contact Kathleen Erickson-Freeman at kfreeman@noetic.org.

The **Legacy of Wisdom** project, based in Switzerland, is dedicated to practical applications of "wise living and aging." A growing video collection (more than two hundred) of "Answers to Key Questions" features eminent and respected generational leaders and is available in its online library. Interviews focus on five main areas of aging: Mission and Fulfillment; Aging Lifestyles and Relationships; Health and Healthcare; Legal and Finances; and End of Life Preparations. Legacy of Wisdom also sponsors conferences and workshops with inspiring elders, and US courses are currently being developed for 2014. www.legacyofwisdom.com

The Life Planning Network is a community of professionals and organizations dedicated to helping people navigate the second half of life. Its mission is to create resources that support professionals in their work to enhance people's later lives, thus benefiting society. Chapters around the country offer regular program opportunities for participants to share and learn from other members. In addition, members collaborate, refer, co-market, and partner in other ways to build their respective businesses and to advance the value of the life planning movement for the benefit of all. Members are invited to promote their organizations and activities to the public through a directory on the LPN website. www.lifeplanningnetwork.org

Memorial BrainWorks is based on the philosophy that brain health is the single most determining factor in quality of life, and that making brain-healthy lifestyle choices is an investment in long-term mind and body resilience. The organization's award-winning program, Grandbuddies, is a mental fitness program for older adults. Memorial BrainWorks sponsors webinars and by-invitation educational programs promoting personal growth and development throughout the elder years, and reaches out to younger people as well to encourage lifestyles that will support healthy aging. www .memorialbrainworks.com

The National Center for Creative Aging (NCCA) fosters an understanding of the vital relationship between creative expression and healthy aging, and works to develop programs that build on this understanding. The process of aging is a profound experience marked by increasing physical and emotional change and a heightened search for meaning and purpose. The arts can serve as a powerful way to engage elders in a creative and healing process of self-expression, enabling them to create works that honor their life experience. www.creativeaging.org

Fruitful Aging and Recognition Rites for Elders, a program founded by Dr. Tom Pinkson, offers a unique blend of ancient and contemporary knowledge that embraces the aging process and older people in general. It brings an intergenerational audience together for a ceremonial honoring of a selected elder that helps break down barriers of separation and builds community. Recognition Rites fosters a greater appreciation of aging and of older people, and serves as a seed and stimulus for those in attendance to create celebrations for themselves or for meaningful elders in their lives. www.drtompinkson.com

Sage-ing® International works to change society's current belief system from aging to sage-ing—that is, from simply becoming old to aging consciously. Believing that the wisdom and gifts of conscious elders are urgently needed in today's world, Sage-ing International offers workshops, elder circles, and Sage-ing workshop leader training programs that support living with passion, purpose, inner growth, and commitment to service. A free six-month Associate Membership is offered on the Sage-ing International website, providing access to valuable resources for individuals wanting to do their own conscious aging work while encouraging others to do likewise. www.sage-ing.org

Second Journey is helping birth a new vision of the rich possibilities of later life, focusing on "Mindfulness, Service, and Community in the Second Half of Life." Workshops and Visioning Councils address individual growth and spiritual deepening, service and mentoring in later life, new models of community, and marshaling the distilled wisdom and experience of elders to address the converging crises of our time. Additional rich resources are offered on the website. Second Journey publishes the excellent online conscious aging journal "Itineraries" and print books such as *Aging In Community* that include "Itineraries" articles and other contributions from thought leaders in conscious aging. www.SecondJourney.org

The Elder Spirituality Project of Spirituality & Practice launched in 2013 with a series of interactive e-courses led by multi-faith spiritual teachers such as Angeles Arrien and Christina Baldwin who are known for their insights into the spiritual blessings and challenges of later life. Participants receive e-courses by email and are invited to create online Practice Circles where they share experiences and insights. In 2014 the Elder Spirituality Project will have a special section of the website for curated content, including program plans for small groups of elders in different settings; reviews of recommended books, DVDs, and audios for and about elders; and a database of quality-of-life spiritual practices for elders from all religions and spiritual paths. www.SpiritualityandPractice.com/ElderSpirituality

NOTES

1: Conscious Eldering:
The Journey to Wholeness As We Age

1. Carl G. Jung, *Modern Man in Search of a Soul* (New York: Routledge, 2001), 111.
2. Frederick Buechner, *Wishful Thinking: A Theological ABC* (San Francisco: Harper, 1993).
3. Bill Plotkin, *Nature and the Human Soul: Cultivating Wholeness and Community in a Fragmented World* (Novato, CA: New World Library, 2008), 394–401.
4. Tom Pinkson, *Fruitful Aging: Finding the Gold In the Golden Years* (San Anselmo, CA: Self-Published, 2013), 33.

2: Life Transitions and Rites of Passage: Portals to Conscious Elderhood

1. John Allan and Pat Dyck, "Transition from Childhood to Adolescence: Developmental Curriculum," in *Betwixt and Between: Patterns of Masculine and Feminine Initiation*, ed. Louise Carus Mahdi, Steven Foster, and Meredith Little (La Salle, IL: Open Court Publishing, 1987), 25.
2. Louise Carus Mahdi, Steven Foster, and Meredith Little, eds., *Betwixt and Between: Patterns of Masculine and Feminine Initiation* (La Salle, IL, Open Court Publishing, 1987).

3: Nature As Healer and Teacher

1. Bill Plotkin, *Nature and the Human Soul: Cultivating Wholeness and Community in a Fragmented World* (Novato, CA: New World Library, 2008).
2. Richard Louv, *Last Child in the Woods: Saving Our Children from Nature-Deficit Disorder* (Chapel Hill: Algonquin Books of Chapel Hill, 2005).

4: No Regrets: Healing the Past to Empower the Future

1. Steve Harsh, "The Family Quilt: Harvesting and Sharing Life's Wisdom," *Itineraries* (Spring 2011): 31–36.

5: The Work of Forgiveness and Grief

1. Elisabeth Kübler-Ross, *On Death and Dying* (New York: Touchstone, 1969).

6: The Power of Story to Shape Our Future

1. Jean Houston, *The Wizard of Us: Transformational Lessons from Oz* (Hillsboro, OR: Beyond Words Publishing, 2012), 12.

7: Shedding Old Skins So We May Grow

1. Ram Dass, *Still Here: Embracing Aging, Changing, and Dying* (New York: Riverhead Books, 2000).
2. Letty Cottin Pogrebin, quoted in *Family Wisdom: The 2,000 Most Important Things Ever Said about Parenting, Children, and Family Life*, compiled by Susan Ginsberg (New York: Columbia University Press, 1996), 76.
3. Zalman Schachter-Shalomi and Ronald S. Miller, *From Age-ing to Sage-ing: A Revolutionary Approach to Growing Older* (New York: Warner Books, 1995), 23.

8: Releasing the Past in the Death Lodge

1. Steven Foster and Meredith Little, *The Roaring of the Sacred River: The Wilderness Quest for Vision and Self-Healing* (New York: Prentice Hall, 1989), 34.
2. Ira Byock, *The Four Things That Matter Most: A Book About Living* (New York: Free Press, 2004), 4–9.

13: Finding Support in Community

1. Janelle Orsi and Emily Doskow, *The Sharing Solution: How to Save Money, Simplify Your Life & Build Community* (Berkeley, CA: Nolo Press, 2009).
2. Anthony Bolton, "Creating Community in Later Life," in *Aging in Community*, ed. Janice M. Blanchard (Chapel Hill, NC: Second Journey Publications, 2013), 20. Anthony borrowed parts of this quotation from Robert N. Bellah et al., *Habits of the Heart: Individualism and Commitment in American Life* (New York: Harper and Row, 1985), 85.